This book opens your eyes to the dynamic blindness that has captured us through-out the years. It earnestly places you in different perspectives and makes you think "what would I do?" It is important that we take a hard look at ourselves and begin the meticulous process of making effective changes in our lives, our loved ones, and humanity.

Finella White
Special Education Teacher
VIDA Educator for Los Angeles Sheriff's Department

The single largest epidemic of our time is the destruction of our children. Unfor-tunately, this disease is being created by parents. If you want to immunize your family from the disaster of failed love and connection in your childhood, then Mark Cripe has finally shared the answer. Admitting that men can be tough, even when frightened and confused, Mark takes the understanding of the "angry 60s parenting model" to REAL healing family connection. Thank God for this insight. Our children might have hope for solid families.

Vicky Thomas, DCH
Author, Ho'oponopono - A Deep and Lasting Forgiveness Process
Master Hypnotist Trainer

Mark has an incisive ability to tap that part of truth that is real to us all . . . as a result, he gently encourages us to live to this potential in all aspects of our lives . . . the humbling reality is made easy by his engaging ability to touch what is right in us long enough for us to remember that it is important and needs our attention.

Brian Mattson, PhD
Justice Analytics, Inc.

PRAISE FOR *LOVE LOUDLY*

Sergeant Cripe's voice is an articulate blend of experience and expertise, culminating in teachable moments for youth advocates and multidisciplinary professionals. Readers will be moved by emotion, leading them to constructive action for children. Love Loudly *provides insight into a world where so many adults need to venture so all children are heard and respected. All children deserve to receive* Love Loudly *and Sergeant Cripe provides us with the critical insight needed to reach children, especially when they appear "unreachable."*

Kathleen Van Antwerp, EdD
Professor of Education and Child and Adolescent Development
Founder, One Circle, Inc. and Knowledge-Based Parenting

This is not a book written by some behavioral PhD or child psychologist looking for more speaking engagements. This is a hard walk through the trenches in the battles we all face as parents. The stories are raw and real, sometimes heartbreaking and sometimes joyful. But if we're honest, kids and parents are sometimes heartbreaking one moment and joyful the next. Cripe takes us through it all with grace and a humility that is missing from every other treatment on the subject. This is not a parenting book but a memoir from a man who has raised three excellent kids of his own plus hundreds of others through the VIDA program. My only regret is not reading this before raising my own four kids.

Mike Barrett
Author of *The Danger Habit* (Random House 2007)
CEO of Unosquare

Sergeant Mark Cripe has a very unique insight coming from years of education, training, and real life experience, both as a valued member of law enforcement and that of an ordinary father, husband, and law-abiding citizen. From the moment you open his book one immediately senses his understanding, support, and commitment to the welfare, hopes, and dreams of other parents and their relationships with their children. Love Loudly *shares Mark's insights, skills, and abilities with others in this most difficult aspect of our world. I know, I have witnessed this first hand myself.*

John Hutak, DPA, Public Administration
Superintendent of Schools (retired)
School Safety and Security Consultant

In my fifteen years as a teacher and advocate of at-risk students, Mark is one of the most empathetic, compassionate, understanding, and genuine people I have had the pleasure to work with. He has such an incredible way of using experiences from his life's journey to relate to those he works with, teaches, and comes in contact with. The two most powerful emotions we have are love and fear. This book can be used as a seedling to assist and develop your emotional tree one branch at a time.

Debbie Billingsley
Special Education Teacher, Utah

Sergeant Mark Cripe, LASD, has written a gripping book that all parents, parenting instructors, and youth should read. It is a "through the looking glass" account of one man's journey to becoming one of the "good ones" who work with at-risk youth (all youth) and their parents, teaching them to have meaningful, healthy relationships with others, especially the ones they love most, and to have useful insight and tools for a successful journey.

This account tells how we can sort our "baggage" to identify the important tools we have attained in life and use those tools to heal what may have first appeared as a fatal wreck, helping to make whole what was thought to be lost.

Mark E. Nathanson, PhD, CDAAC, RAS

LOVE LOUDLY

LESSONS IN FAMILY CRISIS, COMMUNICATION, AND HOPE

MARK C. CRIPE

Writers of the Round Table Press
PO Box 511, Highland Park, IL 60035
www.roundtablecompanies.com

Publisher	**COREY MICHAEL BLAKE**
Executive Editor	**KATIE GUTIERREZ**
Staff Editor	**PAMELA DeLOATCH**
Creative Director	**DAVID CHARLES COHEN**
Director of Operations	**KRISTIN WESTBERG**
Facts Keeper	**MIKE WINICOUR**
Cover Design	**SUNNY DiMARTINO**
Print and Digital Interior Design	**SUNNY DiMARTINO**
Quote Illustrations	**CAROLINE WINEGEART**
Proofreading	**RITA HESS**
Last Looks	**SUNNY DiMARTINO**
Print and Digital Post Production	**SUNNY DiMARTINO**

Printed in the United States of America
First Edition: June 2014
10 9 8 7 6 5 4 3 2 1

Library of Congress Cataloging-in-Publication Data
Cripe, Mark C.
Love loudly: lessons in family crisis, communication, and hope /
Mark C. Cripe.—1st ed. p. cm.
ISBN Paperback 978-1-939418-52-4
ISBN Digital 978-1-939418-53-1
Library of Congress Control Number: 2014940368

RTC Publishing is an imprint of Writers of the Round Table, Inc.
Writers of the Round Table Press and the RTC Publishing logo
are trademarks of Writers of the Round Table, Inc.

I would like to dedicate this book to my mother and father.
There is no such thing as a perfect parent, only those who try to do their best.
My parents' best, whatever it looked like, set me on a course to matter,
to make a difference in this world and for that,
I am truly thankful.

CONTENTS

FOREWORD

What happens to the child whose cries in the night go unattended? What about the kids who feel trapped in their own home? Some of these children will not survive. Other children in these situations will survive but may not thrive. Perhaps your home is not one where the experiences of abuse or neglect occur, but would it surprise you to learn that children can still fail to thrive in homes where their basic needs *are* met? *How is this possible?* As we think about this question, it might be useful to think about our responsibilities as parents. Some would suggest that our primary responsibility is to ensure that our children become successfully self-sufficient. Does this mean helping children get to a point where they can survive, or does it mean helping them get to a point where they can thrive? In either case, this is not necessarily an easy task. Those questions and others will be addressed as you read the pages of this book. Through his story, Mark is able to illustrate biological, psychological, sociological, and theological theories by integrating everyday examples from his own life. In doing so, we are able to get a better sense of how each relationship interaction shapes us at various stages during our life.

Relationships can be challenging and rewarding. Often the relationships that are most challenging and rewarding are those that are closest in proximity. The parent-child relationship provides many examples of this. There is no way to predict how many challenges or rewards each parent-child relationship will have, but you will encounter both. Most of the time, the parent-child relationship is free of conflict. When faced with challenges, parents are generally able to resolve issues and move on. However, there are times when parents are faced with challenges that seem insurmountable. When this happens, our natural response is to rely on familiar resources. When a peaceful resolution is not reached and everyone is frustrated, we might ask ourselves, "How did we get here?" There is no easy answer to this question, but we owe it to our children to try to find the way to a healthy solution. As with most conflict in the parent-child relationship, the central issue is that the child wants to know that he or she matters to you. I recommend that you keep this in mind as you read Mark's story and as you read the lessons at the end of the book.

By sharing the intimate details of his story, Mark has given us the unique opportunity to see how each phase of his life ultimately influences his parenting. If we are willing to take a similar journey to review our own life story, we may discover how the people we have met along the way have helped shape our interactions with children. The patterns, beliefs, values, and views of parenting we hold were communicated to us by someone. Wouldn't it be worth it to find out who it was? This book will help you ask and perhaps answer these and other important questions. You may find the answers to some of the questions painful, but it will be worth it. No matter what your relationship is with your child, in the end, the answers will help you find your way to a more meaningful parenting experience.

Loren M. Hill, PhD
Director, Forensic Training Institute at The Chicago School of
Professional Psychology

ACKNOWLEDGMENTS

I'd like to acknowledge my wife, Melanie, and three children Megan, Matthew, and Madison for teaching me so much about being a loving parent through the imperfections of life. Their love has inspired me to be more than I thought I ever could be.

I would also like to acknowledge all of my supervisors in the Los Angeles County Sheriff's Department for their continued belief in me and for giving me the opportunities to matter in the communities I serve.

And finally, I want to acknowledge the numerous great men and women in my life that made a difference in me. Their influence and love shaped me into who I am today.

WHY DO WE YELL ! HATE you ! AND WHISPER I LOVE you ?

INTRODUCTION

David was only sixteen years old, but he was already headed for trouble. He skipped school nearly every day, choosing instead to hang with gang members in the crime-ridden, southern Los Angeles area of Florence Firestone.

"Help my son," his mother begged.

She had brought him into the Los Angeles County Sheriff's Department, to our juvenile intervention program called VIDA (Vital Intervention and Directional Alternatives), hoping we could change his course. As an L.A. County deputy sheriff and key organizer of this program, I felt sure that over time we could provide the motivation to get David to go to school. Yet as weeks went by and despite our best efforts, we kept getting the same report: David was still skipping school. Didn't he know that he wouldn't pass if he had too many absences? Didn't he know that he wouldn't graduate—never mind go to college—if he couldn't show up for school on a regular basis? I could tell through his participation in our program that although he wasn't highly educated, he was intelligent. He wasn't afraid of struggling in school. Maybe he was just lazy. Maybe he just didn't care how his truancy worried his mother. Maybe it didn't matter to him that he was wasting his life.

One day during a VIDA session, I drew him aside. Resisting the temptation to put him in a headlock and force some sense into him, I asked, "David, what do I need to do to get you to start going to school? How many times are we going to have to cite you?" Maybe I had to threaten him with trouble to make him behave. "Do I have to come to school every day to make sure you're there?"

He stood before me, a skinny boy with deep brown eyes. "Why?" he asked. "Why would I waste time going to school if I'm going to be dead within five years?"

David's simple words struck a heavier blow than any fist could have. No, he was not suffering from a fatal illness, but it occurred to me that he might as well have been. In David's world, kids didn't live much past the age of twenty. Violence and drugs stole their lives so early that even the younger kids, like David, couldn't envision a long-term future. If you're not going to live past twenty, why would a high school degree matter?

I had to take a step back because in this context, what David was doing made complete sense. *I* was the one who wasn't being logical. I had assumed, the way most people might, that I had this kid all figured out. But my paradigm, my view of the world, was clearly not the same as David's was. As long as I continued to try to get kids—particularly those in our juvenile intervention program—to see things my way, I would fail. Our system would fail. We were already seeing that in the sheriff's department. We held the common idea that if we could monitor gang activity or crack down on juvenile delinquency or scare kids straight, they would behave. But it wasn't working.

That day, with David, I began to change. I had to. I had to stop assuming I knew what a kid's life story was. I had to stop assuming I knew the answers. Instead, I had to start learning to ask better questions. And that changed everything. It changed the way I looked at kids. Instead of David being a lazy, shortsighted hoodlum, I now saw him as an insightful and pragmatic youth. Understanding his reasoning helped me change my questions. Instead of asking him why he wasn't going to school, I needed to ask him if he wanted to live past twenty. If he said yes, *then* we could talk about how he could do that.

In twenty-three years as an L.A. County deputy sheriff, I've worked with a lot of kids. Even before that, as a wilderness instructor, I helped kids and adults find their way through literal and figurative forests. I understand the fear that runs through the veins of a kid who has lost his way, just as I understand the terror that a parent or teacher has when fearing a child is lost—either in the forest or to vices in the world.

Too many times, however, we let that fear overshadow our willingness to listen, to ask questions, to operate through love. We seek to stop a behavior instead of first seeking to understand the belief that is the root of that behavior.

I know what it feels like to be "that kid." As a child, I grew up in a dysfunctional family in which I bore the brunt of my mother's unpredictable rage. Now, as a dad to three terrific kids, I also understand the vulnerability parents feel when exposing their precious children to the world. And through my work, helping people navigate the forest—or the juvenile system—I've seen the downstream effects of parental behavior, even the kind with best intentions.

This book is a culmination of this knowledge, which, coupled with my life experiences, forged a fervent belief: when creating, building, or repairing a relationship with kids, *love must speak loudest*. This book suggests a different way to approach parenting kids, whether those kids are studiously on the right path, straying off the path, or have hurtled completely down the wrong one. It provides guidance and real-life insights on how to reach the heart of our kids and truly guide them to a successful adulthood.

Be warned: this book asks a lot. Not just of your kids, but of you. Many people come to me asking me to make their kids change. But just as I learned with David, before I can make a change in someone else's life, I need to alter my own behavior. You, too, will find that your child's behavior will not change until you make changes of your own. Guaranteed, this will require work.

Also guaranteed: it will be worth the effort.

We all just want to BELONG.

BORN IN
FEAR

CHAPTER 1

THE BEDROOM I SLEPT IN AS A CHILD WAS THE LONELIEST AND SCARIEST PLACE IN THE ENTIRE HOUSE. The farthest room from the general living area, the space had a feeling of complete isolation. In the daylight, you could see the many cribs left lined up along the walls from the days my mother and father were foster parents. By night, it was pitch black.

The narrow white wood railings of tonight's crib rattled in the grip of my small hands as I cried for my mom to help me. I had dropped my nightly bottle of warm milk onto the floor, and without that comfort to help me get to sleep, all I could do at first was call for my mother. The cry for help turned into wailing in earnest, and then the wailing turned into begging. Fear soon took over as help-lessness set in. I screamed as loudly as I could, shaking the side of the bed, desperately fighting my reality of complete abandonment.

The door flew open with tremendous force, slamming the knob into the wall with a startling bang. The hallway light revealed the location of my bottle lying on the floor a few feet away, but now the bottle was the least of my worries; I did not even dare to move. The monster had entered the room. Her heavy footsteps indicated her emotional state as she strode over to me, not out of concern but in a rage. This was the woman who had given birth to me, but she was not the mother who had gently put me to bed a short time ago. She seized me, her forty-two-year-old hands squeezing my tiny up-per body like a vice.

"Shut up, shut up, shut up! If you're going to cry, I will give you something to cry about!" she said between her teeth as she shook me. My head bobbled on my toddler-sized neck for what seemed like an eternity as I struggled to look up at her silhouetted face. My frustration and fear had turned into silent terror. Satisfied that I was at last quiet, she let me go, and my legs collapsed. I sank down to the plastic-covered mattress. "Go to sleep!" she commanded, as she strode out the door. Her last statement was her signature, and the slamming of the door once again plunged my room into darkness. My bottle still rested on the floor, and I was completely, hopelessly alone.

In the 1960s, there was no term to describe my childhood other than "normal." It was a time when television was still black and white, when you only had thirteen channels to choose from—if you were lucky—and they all signed off at midnight with a waving American flag and the playing of the national anthem. There were no "dysfunctional families," no child abuse laws, no domestic violence help lines. Of course, that did not mean there was no dysfunction, child abuse, or domestic violence.

As a little boy, I knew how to fear. I was the youngest of five children, living with my parents in a rural neighborhood in the foothills of Los Angeles. I was born ten years after my next closest sibling and twenty years after my oldest. When my siblings moved out of the house at their earliest opportunity, I was trapped at home, essentially an only child.

When I was still a toddler, my parents, Dorothy and Quentin, often had hellacious battles. On one night I can vividly recall, I was wearing one-piece pajamas with the zip front and enclosed feet. This was a well-used pale yellow one, with a hole that let my left big toe poke out. I clutched the thinning cloth diaper that I was allowed to use as a blankie. My parents were screaming and shoving each other as they quickly moved throughout the house. Even though I tried to cover my ears, I could still hear the tones of hatred and rejection they spewed. They fought often, but this one was particularly physical, and I was terrified of what would happen next. I wanted things to be okay, but there was no one in the house big enough to stop it.

I ran into the kitchen, where the only phone in the house clung to the wall far above my head. Even at that age, I knew that you could get an operator to summon the police when you needed help. I reached up to grab the receiver, praying my parents wouldn't notice and turn their anger onto me. I stretched and reached and stood on my tippy toes, but I was too short to lift the phone off the hook. I would not be getting anyone to come for help. I couldn't make it stop. Torn between frustration and panic, I finally gave in to hopelessness. Tears rushed to my eyes at the failure. Forced to accept my insecurity, I turned my back against the wall and slid against the faded sunshine-yellow paint until my bottom rested on the cold, dirty linoleum floor. I lowered my head between my knees, my hands cupped over my ears as I tried to shut out the raging world.

Even when my folks weren't at war, an underlying tension reinforced that things could always spiral out of control without warning. As I aged beyond the toddler years, I wandered the house like a lost soul, searching for a safe place to sleep. It was rarely in my bed. Rather, I rested behind the living room couch, in a corner . . . anywhere hidden where no one could predict where I was.

Although my parents could get physical with each other, my dad never physically hit me. Instead, he put me down verbally. "You're stupid," he often told me. "You'll never amount to anything." In a way, that meant the pressure was off. When I was in eighth grade, I was failing math, despite having excelled in Advanced Placement math the year before. Some parents might have been concerned that their previously advanced son's grades had sunk so low. They might have sat down with me at night to go over homework. They might have made an appointment to talk to the algebra teacher who had destroyed my desire to *try* to learn. But not in my house. Why bother? I wasn't expected to succeed, so when I didn't, I was just fulfilling their expectations. The only adult to step up and offer positive reinforcement in my life was my older sister, Karen. She often told me—kindly—that I could do better, and her belief in me was just enough to carry me through a very lonely time.

As an adult, I see that there is a difference between not caring and not knowing how to care. I believe that my parents did not know how to care. I do not think it was ever modeled to them. All my parents knew was how to fear. As I look back upon those times, I'm not sure what they feared concretely, but I guess it was fear of rejection; fear of failure. In order not to feel those emotions, they opted not to try. As a result, I can tell you that rejection, not love, was spoken the loudest in my home. My childhood questions went unanswered, or answered with a "No" or "Because I said so." Mom and Dad constantly made negative statements to each other and to me that promoted insecurity. When one of the kids asked my father why he never told our mother he loved her, he replied: "I told her I loved her when I married her and if I changed my mind, I'd let her know." Dad often told me that I didn't have the common sense I was born with and that I was too stupid to amount to anything. I never had anything resembling a conversation about life direction, success, or dreams with my mother or father. No wonder there was so much fear in me when love seemed absent most of the time. It's not surprising that I formed a belief, deep down, that my dreams did not matter, that my life did not matter, and that *I* did not matter. I had learned how to live in fear from the adults who were supposed to teach me about love.

By the time I finally started to sleep in my bed, which had been moved to the garage when I was four so my parents could use my bedroom, other issues arose. For years after, I would wake up and stick my hand under the covers to check the mattress. Damn. The bedding was wet again. My pajamas were wet and clammy as I stripped them off, hoping that through some miracle, the embarrassing problem would just go away. My mother knew about the issue, and her answer was to cram a large spoonful of honey into my mouth every night before I went to sleep—one of her many "from the farm" remedies. No one was there to explain that for kids like me, who grow up in chaos and uncertainty, bedwetting is a common response. Indeed, it's a red flag of possible abuse. Even when I reached nine years old, I felt shame that I couldn't stay dry during the night.

You'd think that now, as an adult, I'd leave these memories, this shame and insecurity, behind, yet they affect me to this day. Because of the abuse around and toward me, I never felt I fit in. I never encountered any form of validation. I did not learn how to be secure in who I was. Any form of attention was better than no attention, so as a child, I behaved poorly and immaturely, proving that I was worthy of the rejection I received and which tormented me each day.

. . .

Sometimes I wonder what led to my parents' apparent hatred of each other. After all, their relationship, as I perceived it, was not a love/hate relationship. It was mostly hate/hate.

My mother was a first generation immigrant from Russia, originally from Germany. My dad's family came to the United States in 1722 and became German Mennonite farmers. My mom was the oldest of eight, and when she and Dad met and started dating, she thought marriage would be a way to escape being the babysitter to her seven younger siblings; I heard her say this on several occasions. I think my dad actually loved her, in the beginning at least, but she never seemed happy with him. Of course, if she expected to be child-free, it didn't happen. My sister Linda came very shortly after they married, and Karen was born two years later. There was a huge gap before Jerry and Lisa were born, followed by another ten-year gap, and then there was me.

Maybe Mom was bitter about the way life had turned out for her, or maybe she developed other mental or emotional issues, but she was clearly unhappy. As a child, however, I experienced that unhappiness as constant inconsistency between a mother who loved me and a mother who hated me. On the one hand, she would take me grocery shopping at the local Ralph's. If I were a "good boy," I would get to pick out one Matchbox car. She would give me big hugs and say, "You're my gift from God." On the other hand, she beat me with anything she could lay her hands on, and if she couldn't reach me, she threw things at me. I learned to make her chase me so that when she started beating me she was already winded and the blows wouldn't be as hard.

People talk about the need to discipline children, but this wasn't discipline; this was punishment through a rage so great it made her breathless. Most of the time, I had no clue why I was beaten. I admit it: growing up, I was an obnoxious smartass, trying to gain acceptance through humor, but really, I was a typical kid. Still, when I misbehaved, there was no discussion. I was beaten or shunned, and I was put in my room or a corner for hours. There was no compassion, no seeking understanding, no *My Three Sons* or *Leave it to Beaver* bonding moment where the parents explained their reasoning or intentions. Even as a child, I told myself that I wouldn't be this kind of parent to my own children.

When I was growing up, little was researched or known about child abuse, even by the medical community. Not until 1972 did the majority of states enact laws governing the reporting of child abuse. But those changes didn't make a difference in my life. Our neighbors never seemed to perceive the noise at our house as abuse. And my parents never sought help or parenting guidance from Dr. Spock.

While their behavior sometimes seemed to be sparked by frustration, other times it just seemed intentionally cruel. When I was ten, I wanted a bike more than anything for Christmas. We weren't well off by any means. In fact, we were poor, but I wasn't thinking about that when I asked for a bike. I just wanted the freedom it would give me to ride around the neighborhood with my friends. It was a chance to feel like a normal kid, so I begged and nagged my dad for one. Birthdays were never a big deal in our house, but as every kid knows from any holiday television show, Christmas offers magical possibilities, so this particular year, I hoped.

Sure enough, one afternoon when we were in the living room, Dad said he had a surprise for me. "Come here, I've got something to show you," he said.

Barely containing my excitement, I matched my footsteps with his as I followed him out of the house and around to the side of the garage. Dad opened the big wooden door and pointed to a pile of metal pieces. "There's your bike. Now you can build any bike you want."

My eyes struggled to focus. It wasn't a bike! It was a stack of junk, mismatched pieces from different bikes: a banana seat, parts of a ten-speed, and bits from a Schwinn. Dad had gone around the neighborhoods picking out bike parts from neighbors' trash. Without instructions or a manual (and there was certainly no help desk or Internet), he unceremoniously gave me the pile to work with and walked away.

For a long time, I was sure this was just a colossal joke. Ha! Kid thinks he's getting a bike. Let's give him a pile of junk instead—see what he makes of that! But once I breathed away the tears of anger and frustration, I decided to figure out exactly how to make a bike, despite my dad never offering to help me. I ended up going with a boy's bike with a banana seat. I painted it red because I wanted to be a fireman. The bike had no brakes, so when my friends and I rode downhill, I followed, knowing that I would probably crash at the bottom, which I did quite a bit. Once my bike was built, my dad never said anything about it, never asked to see it, and certainly never commended me on my work. When I look back, I think that maybe Dad was trying to teach me a life lesson about making something for myself. But it took years of hurt feelings before I even considered that as a possibility.

Riding my bike gave me a much-needed respite from my mom. One Sunday, after church service ended, I saw something that represented even more freedom.

One of the meeting room doors was open just wide enough that I could see boys bustling around inside, dressed in tan shirts with cool patches, green shorts, and brown lace-up boots. Dozens of backpacks lay on a table, and the excited chatter within drew me closer.

"Who are they?" I murmured as I lingered near the door.

"Boy Scouts," a passerby said.

Boy Scouts. I could almost smell the adventure. These guys were going backpacking and camping and would get to go places far away from everything! It was the coolest thing I could imagine, and I yearned to join them in that room. As I stood at the doorway, a tall man approached me from inside.

"Hello, son. Are you a Boy Scout?" he asked.

I shook my head.

"How old are you?" he asked kindly.

"Ten," I responded.

"You have to be twelve to be a Boy Scout. Come back in a few years," he said. With a wink, he gently closed the door.

My shoulders slumped. It would be *forever* before I turned twelve. As much as I had wanted a bike, I wanted this even more.

For the next two years, I begged my parents to let me join Scouts. I was still too young to go, of course, but my parents sent me off to camps and activities whenever they could—not because I wanted to participate in those things but to get me out from underfoot. One year, my mother paid five dollars for me to go to a weeklong camp in the Angeles Crest National Forest.

But as much as I asked to join the Scouts, I knew it wasn't going to happen. We just didn't have the money. For one thing, we'd have to buy equipment, like those backpacks I had seen on the table at church. My mom was now working as a babysitter, treating other people's kids the way she treated her own, but we still didn't have a lot to spare. My mom sewed my school clothes to save money, and I often wore shoes held together with duct tape. I couldn't help it, though. Every time I saw someone in his Boy Scout uniform on the street or passed the group at church, I wanted a piece of what they had. That confidence, that camaraderie. That sense of purpose and belonging.

Finally, I turned twelve, and even though I still asked to join Scouts, I did it more out of habit than because I actually thought it would happen.

Then, one Saturday, Mom and I were driving to a store when she casually asked me if I still wanted to join Scouts.

"Yes!" I exclaimed.

She nodded.

Was this a trick? Was she just asking so that she could then respond, "Well, you're not going to!" Or even if I did join, would she make me sew my own backpack? But for a reason I will never know, my mom had decided I should join Boy Scouts.

One Monday night, after one of my Scout meetings, my mother headed our beat-up blue Plymouth hatchback in the wrong direction. I looked out the window, confused. Weren't we going home? She pulled into the parking lot of the Burbank Big 5 store, and slowly my confusion morphed into excitement in my chest. I held my breath, knowing not to expect anything.

When we entered the store, Mom announced that she was going to buy me a backpack and a sleeping bag. I could not believe it: I was going to get to pick out a brand new backpack of my own! I chose a dark green Camp Trails pack just like the other boys had. I ran my fingers over the stitching and jumped up to try it on, shrugging my shoulders to feel its weight. Finally, I looked at my mom, who watched me with an unreadable expression.

"Thanks, Mom," I said, lost in amazement and gratitude.

"Don't tell your father I used my babysitting money for this," she responded.

I tried to hold my composure until we got home and I reached my bedroom. There, with no one to witness my joy, I hugged my new backpack to my chest. I zipped and unzipped each pocket, discovering each compartmental mystery. I inhaled the backpack's scent and chortled to myself with glee. Somehow I knew, as I had known when I was ten, that being part of Scouts would transition me out of the inferno I had been living in. What I did not know was how many doors it would open for my future.

ANY MOMENT CAN BE A Teaching moment OF IMPACT

AT HOME
IN THE
WILD
ERNESS

· CHAPTER 2 ·

SOMETIMES, RELATIONSHIPS COME INTO OUR LIVES THAT HAVE THE ABILITY
TO COUNTER THE NEGATIVE INFLUENCES HOLDING US CAPTIVE. These types
of relationships are identified as "strengths" in today's criminogenic
risk assessments. For me, Mr. Bill Ruth and Mr. Rodger Rangler
were two strengths that forged a monumental shift in my life.

Even though I'm probably as old now as they were when we
first met, I always think of them by the title of *Mister*. Not out of
fear, but out of respect. Both men were the leaders of my very first
Scout troop. They were instrumental in helping me learn what it
meant to be a good Scout and, eventually, a good person. This was
the first time I was exposed to concepts like leadership, teamwork,
servanthood, morals, ethics, support, and affirmations. For the first
time, I saw that being the head of a group didn't mean browbeating,
shouting, manipulating, or shaming everyone into behaving.

My first Scout meeting was surreal. I was not only inside the
room I had stolen a peek into a few years earlier, but I was also sitting with many of those same boys. I could hardly believe it: I was
one of them now!

"Mark." Mr. Ruth put his hand on my shoulder. Startled, I looked up at him. He smiled. "Welcome to the troop. We are glad to have you here."

As excited as I was to finally be at a Scouts meeting, I was also anxious. I was smaller than the other boys and figured I was younger, too. Would they let me into their circle? Would I be able to do what they did?

After Mr. Ruth walked away, one boy turned toward me. "Hey," he said in greeting. He shifted over and, just like that, included me.

A few minutes later, the Scout leaders called the meeting to order, and at last I got to recite the Boy Scout oath: "On my honor, I will do my best to do my duty to God and my country and to obey the Scout law; to help other people at all times; to keep myself physically strong, mentally awake, and morally straight."

My heart pounded as I awkwardly spoke those words, my index finger and middle finger proudly raised in the Scout sign. Quite suddenly, I had a responsibility. To God. To my country. To the group of Scouts. Me—the kid who was continually told he was stupid and would never amount to anything. The kid who always felt he was a burden. I now had a purpose.

The meeting started, as they all did, with troop business: roll call, announcements, and so on. I was like a sponge, soaking up every second. My excitement was almost more than I could control, my feet tapping the ground unstoppably (a behavior that often got me in trouble at home).

I had so much to learn in an environment that was completely foreign that I survived the first meeting by mimicking what the other boys did. As lost as I felt, the huge smile on my face broadcasted that a dream was coming to life.

I loved the weekly Scout meetings. I loved having purpose, having a role. I loved the structure, from the pre-meeting social time to the opening ceremony to the skill-building instruction and patrol meetings and activities. Most of all, I loved feeling alive when we went on hikes.

The day of my first real backpacking trip, Mom dropped me off in front of our church, where the troop regularly met. It was a

Saturday morning, and I had risen from bed well before the sun. This was the day, the dream was alive, and I was actually going to do it! I stood there as Mom pulled away, my backpack already heavy on my thin shoulders, and I breathed the moment into my soul.

Once everyone had arrived, we all loaded up in the van and headed out towards the foothills of northern Los Angeles County. We bounced and brimmed with excitement, rowdy and somewhat unruly. The van pulled up to the trailhead, and we all bailed out.

This was going to be a short and simple hike, just a two-mile stroll. As I look back, I would say that the area was boring: no trees, no hills to ascend and descend, no lakes. Just a flat, dry, dusty trail that went nowhere, but the air was clean and crisp, and as I inhaled, I felt as if it cleaned me inside. The mountains towered over me in all directions, but instead of making me feel small, they enveloped me, welcoming me with open arms.

"Okay, boys." Mr. Ruth called us all together. "This is our first hike of the season. Who remembers the rules?"

I raised my hand quickly, remembering to wait to answer until I was acknowledged.

"Mark?"

"Stay with a buddy, and if you have to go off the trail to pee, leave your backpack on the trail," I answered.

"That's right," Mr. Ruth nodded. "Good job."

I ducked my head, not wanting anyone to see my face flush awkwardly at the words of commendation. I hadn't received such positive recognition before. But Mr. Ruth believed in telling us when we did or said the right thing, and even when we didn't, both he and Mr. Rangler excelled at using calm voices that demanded respect. We wanted to please them.

After reviewing the remaining rules and the path, we set out. The older boys set the pace as we gradually climbed higher, and I scrambled to keep up with them. My backpack was newbie-packed. It held the necessities, such as a sleeping bag, a basic insulated sleeping pad, a ground cloth, group food, water, my Scout pocketknife, and extra clothes, but I had packed stupid stuff as well, like metal utensils and rope used for clotheslines. Sure, we had gone over what to bring and what not to bring, but as I packed, I thought, surely I could take this or that. I had created in my mind the needs of a boy in the woods.

It did not take long for the weight of the pack to educate me about many things in life: the importance of lightening our burdens the best we can, the power of resiliency, and the one-step-more mindset. I learned to differentiate between needs and wants, and learned why we were instructed to only take what we needed. After all, a burden may feel easy if you only have to carry it for a moment, but if you are traveling any distance with it, you'd better count its cost. This pack, which felt so light when I had stuffed it the night before, grew heavier and heavier. My shoulders burned as the straps dug into them through my shirt. I knew nothing about adjusting my pack to my little body, so some of the older boys helped me on the trail. They tightened this strap and loosened that one until it all fit right, albeit still too heavy.

Although the morning temperature was cool, sweat now dripped into my eyes. With my short, shuffling steps, I caught up to the lead group just in time to watch them take off again. My legs screamed as I forced myself to lengthen my stride to keep up with the older boys, and other areas of my wimpy body soon joined in the complaining. This hike was turning into an exercise of enduring more pain than I had ever felt before. It was the first time I'd ever pushed my muscles to perform.

"Let's take a break," said Kevin Stacy. Kevin was everything I wasn't. Standing around six feet tall, he had shoulder-length dirty blond hair and deep blue eyes. As one of the older boys and Senior Scouts, he stuck out his freckled arm and pointed to a shady clearing about a hundred feet ahead. When we reached it, I lowered my backpack to the ground and tried not to groan in relief. Furtively, I stretched my stiff shoulders and then noticed the other boys were stretching and rubbing their shoulders, too. I sat down on the ground and opened my backpack to pull out my canteen of water. At the bottom of the backpack, along with my canteen, was a container of powered Gatorade. Mom must have put that in there, and I was grateful, though plain water would have tasted like heaven, too.

"Hey, you've got Gatorade?" Kevin asked, looking over at my container. "Can I have some?"

I shrugged. "Sure," I said, playing it cool as I handed him the container. Just the fact that he noticed my existence was amazing! He opened his canteen and the Gatorade and carefully poured the powdery mix into his water. Then he replaced the top on his canteen and shook it, opening it again to take a drink.

"Ahh," he said, wiping his mouth and grinning. "This is good. My mom always gives me Tang." Kevin took a moment to engage me in small talk and then suggested that I hike along with him up front. "Do you think you can keep up?"

I truly doubted that I could, but I was going to will my little skinny legs to go.

Over the next several hikes, Kevin taught me how to lengthen my stride and how to consciously relax other muscles through the stride. Neither he nor I realized that he was teaching me something that would pay dividends later in my life, both as a professional wilderness leader and an infantry Marine. Yes, I kept up!

From then on, the older boys assumed that I would hike along with them, leaving boys more my age and size in the back of the group. Each hike, I had a full container of Gatorade that I shared with the group, and afterward, I had so little my mother must have thought I'd emptied it out along the trail. The random kindnesses she showed me from time to time confused me, but I soaked them up. To this day, I am thankful to her, because without her occasional generosity, I would have never started to backpack, and backpacking was a catalyst for so much in my life.

My knowledge and confidence grew during those first years in Scouts. As my shoulder sash filled up with merit badges, my self-concept also took shape. Instead of hearing "You're stupid" or "You will not amount to anything," I was now hearing different messages: "You've become a really strong hiker" or "Good job, Mark," or even "That's a good try." Here, I wasn't a failure. I saw a different truth: I mattered, I belonged, and I was accomplishing things I never thought I could.

· · ·

In our troop, we could earn the privilege of going on longer and longer hikes. We earned this opportunity—and for me, it was indeed an opportunity—by following the rules during the troop meetings, working hard at building our skill levels, and showing ability on the shorter hikes. The biggest hike of the year was a six-day trip in the High Sierras, where we hiked forty to sixty miles in high elevations. We even picked off Mount Whitney on one trip, where the summit is 14,505 feet above sea level. The more often I hiked, the more I realized I was good at it. My body grew strong as I learned to balance the weight of my backpack against my own body weight on the shifting trail. I learned to watch the weather on the horizon, how to find the best place to camp for the night, and what elements could do me harm. Most importantly, I learned how to stay safe while cohabitating with the wildlife.

The idea of coming across a bear or a snake in the woods didn't scare me. At home, I couldn't anticipate how my parents would react, what mood they would be in, what might anger them. It was different in the wilderness. The rules of the forest held fast: Never come between a cub and its mother. Don't set the forest on fire. Don't pee in the water, as you may need that water downstream. Follow the simple rules and everything will be fine. As it happened, being in the wild felt a lot safer for me than being in my own home.

Because I respected my Scout leaders so much, I never wanted to disappoint them; but one time, I did.

We were on a twenty-mile hike, one we'd been on before. This time, though, the trail disappeared under huge snow banks. My backpack was heavy, at least twenty-five pounds. The trail got increasingly steep and slippery as we climbed, and the weight of my backpack pulled me backward even as I leaned forward to gain footing. I tried to step in the stomped-in footprints of the bigger boys who were ahead of me. As I took a step, my foot slipped and my heart rate immediately skyrocketed.

"Mark! Watch out!" Wade, a fellow Scout, called as he glanced behind and saw me stumble.

My arms flailed as I tried to regain my balance, but it was too late. I tumbled down the trail we had just painstakingly climbed. As I fell, I twisted and turned, trying to catch myself, but sliding down the slope until I collided with a tree trunk. The backpack took the brunt of the impact on my back, but I hit the tree trunk ribs first. At that impact, I finally lay still, face down in the dirt.

"Mark? Are you okay?" Wade, along with fellow Scouts James and Rob, scrambled down to squat next to me.

I was breathless, completely winded.

"Here, buddy." Wade eased the straps of the backpack down my arms. "Let's get this off. You okay, man?"

"Let's turn him over," James said.

"No!" I managed in a wheeze. "Give me a minute." I waited a few breaths. "Okay, help me get up."

Wade put his hand on my shoulder to turn me over. As I slowly began to rotate, a sharp pain radiated from the ribs on my left side.

"Argh!" I yelled, collapsing back on the ground. Black dots danced in front of my eyes, and I felt the water and peanut butter sandwich I had eaten at our last rest stop threaten to climb back up. Eyes closed, breathing shallowly, I could hear the guys murmuring.

"What are we going to do?" Rob asked, looking up and down at the empty trail.

"Let's get Mr. Rangler," James suggested.

"No. I'll be okay," I said, trying to sound more sure than I felt. I took a few more careful breaths, willing myself to my pain and panic despite the sheet of sweat breaking out on my forehead.

Take inventory, Mark, I thought. My head was okay. Good. My legs were fine. I wiggled my toes to make sure. Arms? I moved them slightly and wiggled my fingers. Good. All the pain was centered in my side. Cracked ribs, I reasoned. I'd had broken bones before and toughed it out, so I knew that even though it hurt, I could get through it. Slowly, a degree at a time, I rolled myself over, resting on my back. Wade, James, and Rob looked down at me anxiously.

Through squinted eyes, I met their gaze. "I'm okay. Let me sit up." I nodded to Wade and held a hand against my ribs as he moved behind me and guided me up until I was sitting. Tears sprang to my eyes from the pain, but I blinked so they wouldn't fall.

"I still think we should tell the Scout leader," James insisted.

"No," I snapped. "It will be all right. I'm just a little banged up. I'll be all right," I repeated. If we told the Scout leaders, I would disappoint them. They would think I wasn't careful enough and shouldn't be helping lead the other Scouts. They might not let me hike with them next time. No, I decided. This would be just between the other Scouts and me.

Somehow, I slowly stood up and we continued the climb, resting every ten minutes. The other guys emptied my backpack and distributed the contents among them, so I only had my canteen. Still, I could only creep along. Using my left arm to help brought a wave of pain that left me breathless. But the guys kept encouraging me, and I kept going.

We finished the climb and made our way back to camp. I stayed on the periphery of the group, and none of the leaders noticed anything wrong. After the trip was over, I gratefully returned home and wrapped my bruised and discolored side, which made moving much easier. I thought I had gotten away with my mishap until a week later, at the next Scout meeting.

"Mark, I want to talk to you," Mr. Rangler said seriously. He motioned me toward him, and he and I stepped out into the hallway away from the meeting. "I know you got hurt during the last hike," he said.

My first instinct was to deny it. I opened my mouth, but then I looked into his eyes and fell silent.

"I'm disappointed in you, son," he said.

"Yes, sir," I responded, looking down so he wouldn't see the blush of shame that washed my face.

"Mark," Mr. Rangler said gently. "Do you know why I'm disappointed?"

"Because I was careless," I responded.

"Mark. Everyone makes mistakes. But you were hurt, and you didn't come to your Scout leaders for help. You could have been seriously injured, with a broken rib, a punctured lung, or internal bleeding, but you lied to us," he said.

"I didn't lie," I protested. "I just didn't tell."

Mr. Rangler let that weak excuse hover in the air for a moment. "And," he continued, "you let your fellow Scouts be complicit in your 'not telling.' Can you imagine how they would feel if something had happened to you? Can you imagine how I would have felt if something had happened to you? Don't you know that you matter?"

Mr. Rangler's words made me pause. I hadn't thought of how my actions affected the people around me and had never anticipated that they might feel some sense of guilt or responsibility or sorrow if I was hurt. It was a foreign concept—one I certainly wasn't used to from my parents. But it laid a tiny little seed in me that maybe Mr. Rangler was right and that, in some way, I did matter. I nodded in acknowledgment, and Mr. Rangler let me go back to my meeting. And I never lied or "didn't tell" again.

I had been a Scout for a couple of years when one day, before our weekly meeting, Mr. Ruth and Mr. Rangler pulled me aside.

"Mark, we'd like you to work with some of the other boys," Mr. Ruth said.

"We would like you to be a patrol leader," Mr. Rangler added.

I nodded. I wasn't quite sure what I was getting myself into, but as I looked into Mr. Ruth's soft blue eyes and Mr. Rangler's bold brown ones, I knew I couldn't disappoint these men who had so strongly conferred their belief in me.

I was sent into one of the small side rooms off of the main meeting room to wait for my new patrol members. One by one, they entered the room. All of them were older and looked rougher than me. They were sulky, snide, and not at all excited about the many opportunities that Scouts could offer them. In other words, they were typical teenagers just wanting to have fun. I sat there wondering how this was going to work out. I had never led anything, let alone a group, and by the time the last boy had walked in, the group was already in goof-off mode.

My first act of leadership was to get this unlikely group to come together and pick a name and a patrol patch. It sounded easy, but two of the older boys were deeply engaged in a whisper-fest, and the others looked bored, no doubt already planning a more exciting activity for when the meeting ended. For a moment, I frowned, irritated and afraid of getting in trouble for not doing what we were told. My first leadership endeavor was more like controlled chaos than anything else. However, we managed to choose the name "Wolverines" and pick a patrol patch (a badger) from the all-knowing *Boy Scout Handbook*. My success may not have been groundbreaking, but it was progress.

During the patrol group meeting, my father's words rang faintly in my head. "Useless. You're worthless. You're stupid and won't ever amount to anything anyway." He had said those words to me repeatedly throughout my childhood. But he was wrong. He never knew me. My Scout leaders knew me better than my own father did, and they saw more potential in me than he ever did. Maybe they saw potential in these "ruffians," too, and if they did, maybe I should pay attention. I shifted from foot to foot as I continued to contemplate the group from across the room. I could assume these guys were hooligans, and maybe they were. But it was possible that their appearances didn't tell the whole story. I could be like my dad and not give them a chance, or I could choose another way. I chose to believe in them—and I told them that. They would be an outstanding troop, I said, and I was looking forward to being their patrol leader. At first, I did not know if this approach would work; all I knew was that I was not going to do to those boys what my dad had done to me.

As I fumbled through facilitating a group decision, I learned quickly about group ownership: the more the group talked and the less I instructed, the more they owned their choices. My job actually became easier, and everyone seemed not only happy but also proud. More importantly, I saw that defining my expectation for their success made something magical happen: they embraced it. Like me, these boys wanted to be recognized; they wanted to be accepted for who they were. They needed someone, anyone, to believe in them, and when I told them I did, right off the bat, we were able to grow together. We began to believe in ourselves. As the year went on, I had the best group of guys. They were willing to work hard and work together, and we had many great hikes as a team.

In those early Scout years, as I grew in confidence, I also grew in height. Without even noticing, I grew three inches between seventh grade and ninth grade. Hiking the hills with heavy backpacks left me with surprisingly strong muscles and a perpetual tan. But although I was a leader in Scouts, I was still just a snotty, obnoxious kid at home. I had a quick mind combined with a smart mouth, and that often got me in trouble.

One afternoon after school, I was rummaging through the refrigerator, looking for a snack that met my teenage standards, when Mom said something to me. To this day, I don't remember what it was, and I don't remember what I said back. What I do remember is the argument that ensued. In these heated exchanges, my mother would become so enraged that she threw whatever was near her at me. In the past, she had thrown knives, cast-iron skillets, pots, and large metal spoons, so as the argument grew louder (and they always did), I moved farther away from her. (One thing I learned was that distance is good when you expect incoming objects.)

My mom glared at me with hate in her eyes. "Just get out!" she yelled. She reached behind her and grabbed a can off the counter. As she raised it over her head, I could see that it was Campbell's Chunky Beef Soup. Without warning, she heaved it at my head. I ducked, but I didn't need to: her aim was so notoriously bad that the can hit the wall two feet away from me, leaving a dent and just missing the grandfather clock. As the can fell onto the carpeted dining room floor, I gaped at my mother in disbelief.

Her eyes widened. Maybe she realized she had gone too far, and for a moment, we just stared at each other. For so many years, I had longed for some kindness, some warmth, some love from her. Occasionally, like when she bought me Matchbox cars or took me to Scouts, I got it. But more likely, I got hit, smacked, slapped, pushed, and yelled at. And I still hoped she would show me the love a little boy deserved. But on that day, she threw a friggin' can of soup at my head!

I had reached my breaking point. As she charged toward me, I leaned over and picked up the can. There must have been an unfamiliar look on my face, because she immediately changed direction and hustled away from me. Without thinking, I started towards her, arm cocked as if to send the can flying at her head. My aim, I guarantee, would be better. Mom emitted a squeak, falling to the floor as if she had already been hit. Crumpled before me, covering her head with her hands, she was like the monster that no longer exists once the lights are turned on, once the bad dream is over.

She was not a monster. She was only a scared child herself.

My anger gave way to something else, and I knew in that moment that I could never actually hurt her.

Silently, I stepped closer to her. She cringed. I bent down, set the can of soup beside her hand, and walked out.

We never spoke about that incident, but Mom never physically hurt me again. I may have still been a kid, but on that day, exercising both strength and restraint, I knew my life was changing.

slow is smooth
SMOOTH is FAST

BECOMING ONE OF "THE FEW, THE PROUD"

CHAPTER 3

IN MY SENIOR YEAR OF HIGH SCHOOL, I WALKED INTO THE LIVING ROOM AND SAW MOM AND DAD STANDING TOGETHER. Mom's expression was strained, and Dad wore his serious look.

"You're going to have to pay rent when you turn eighteen," Dad announced.

For a moment, we stood in silence as I stared at them both. I was surprised, but it should not have come as a shock to me. All of my siblings had gotten the hell out of Dodge as soon as they could. Karen and Linda had moved out and gotten married before they were twenty. My folks kicked Jerry out at sixteen, and Lisa moved in with a friend near the same age. It was simply not a "child-friendly" home.

During the encounter, Mom never said anything. I could see that the two of them had argued about something before I arrived, and I can only imagine it had something to do with Dad's demand. I didn't know it at the time, but my mom had set a magical moment when she, too, was going to leave, and that moment was when the last child was gone from the home. Dad's announcement may have taken her by surprise and forced her to reevaluate her plans. (A few years later, after forty-one years of marriage, she called it quits and left.)

I faced my dad and heard myself start to talk through the huge emotional lump that had risen from my stomach and to my throat. I could feel myself tremble. "Well, if I am going to pay rent, then I am going to live where I want to live." My defiance was a knee-jerk reaction, not at all as confident as it may have sounded. I was caught in a choice of flight, fight, or submit. At that moment, my feelings of rejection and hurt gave way to my anger and contempt, but my lack of courage caused me to fight for a moment and then run.

"Fine with me," Dad snorted. "I don't know how you're going to do that!"

I walked past both of my parents and out the front door. For the first time, I had actually declared my desire for independence to the very people I had been dependent upon my whole life . . . and it terrified me. My time in this dysfunctional nest was coming to an end, but I had done nothing to prepare for the next chapter in my life. I had no plan and very little money. In that moment, I was a dreamer without a dream. But I had spent seventeen years being beaten, insulted, or, at best, ignored, and now my father wanted me to pay for that privilege? No way!

In the weeks that followed, still months before my eighteenth birthday, home life degraded into moments of extreme awkwardness. With school activities, Scouts, and more freedom to spend time with friends, I stayed away as much as possible. When I was there, I stayed in my garage bedroom, making occasional forays into the kitchen and ducking both of my parents as much as possible. The reality was, though, that this house was all that I knew. No matter how dysfunctional it was, it was my norm. It had been my anchor in society, and now I acted like it was no big deal to just let it go.

I was caught in limbo, somewhere between anger and hurt. Knowing that I did not matter was painful enough, but something went deeper: the way I saw it, Mom and Dad were more worried about money than my future or well-being. That ignited a cord of anger deep in my gut, and I swore that I would leave that house as soon as possible, no matter how afraid I was of the uncertain future.

• • •

"You should move in with me," said my best friend, Lee "Shep" McColm, later that night. We sat in his bedroom, each chugging on one of those green glass barrel-like bottles of Mickey's Big Mouths, filled with fine malt liquor.

"Seriously?" I asked.

"Sure," Shep said. "My folks aren't living here. Mom moved in with her friend. Dad's with his girlfriend and just drops by to bring groceries. It's just my sister and me. You could stay here." Shep gestured to his bedroom, which had the same mountain range of dirty clothes piles as mine. "In fact, why wait until you're eighteen? You could move in now."

It wasn't the first time Shep had come to my rescue. We met in junior high, when I was a small, insecure, terrified kid whose timid demeanor screamed, "Bully me!" Raul, a tall, skinny eighth grader with the beginning of a mustache, happily obliged. One day as I was trying to scurry past Raul and his friends after my physical education class, he said something to his friends and laughed. Next thing I knew, he grabbed me from behind.

"What are you doing? Put me down!" I squeaked as Raul picked me up so high that my feet dangled six inches above the floor.

Raul laughed as he strode over to a big trashcan and turned me upside down to dump me in. All of my books fell to the ground, landing as haphazardly as I now dangled.

"Hey, quit that!" a boy's calm voice commanded. Raul paused, still holding me by the ankles. My thin body threatened to slide out of my jeans as I wriggled helplessly, and I grabbed my waistband with one hand and the lip of the trashcan with the other.

"I said, leave him alone," the boy repeated, closer this time.

"Why do you care?" Raul demanded.

"That isn't right and you know it. Leave him alone," the boy said.

Raul sighed and reluctantly flipped me back onto my feet.

"Just having a little fun with the dweeb." He laughed as he gave me a final shove and walked off with his friends.

As the blood rushed back out of my head, I straightened my clothes and shook my hair out of my face. Then I looked up. Who was this kid, and why had he chosen to intervene on my behalf?

Shep stood there, taking my measure. He was taller than me, but then again, at that age, most people were. His shaggy, dirty blond hair gave him a Shaun Cassidy look, and he wore his jeans and plain tee shirt with a simple confidence I lacked. Shep had a well-built upper body and a presence that told everyone he could and would take care of himself.

"I'm Shep," he said.

"Mark," I replied.

"Why was Raul doing that?"

"His name is Raul? You know him?"

Shep nodded.

Without further discussion, we both walked to my class. Shep took me under his wing after that. I wasn't sure why. Maybe he saw that we shared a goofy sense of humor, the same snarky view of the world, or maybe it was something else. I didn't question it. I simply said yes when he invited me to hang out. Over the next weeks and months, he became my best friend. The kids at school respected him—maybe because he seemed more mature than the rest of us without being bossy—and with him as my ally, I stopped being bullied and went back to being ignored.

By high school, I was hanging out with Shep at school and at his house all the time. He would only come to my house to pick me up or if Mom and Dad were gone. I was always too embarrassed to have friends over, dreading either of my parents saying something that could humiliate me. I had come late in my parents' life. My mom and dad were the same age as most of my friends' grandparents were. They knew nothing of my generation, and they didn't care to learn. This lack of understanding created awkward moments for my friends when Mom and Dad would scathingly comment about something they thought was ridiculous. Without talking about it, Shep understood. He was my brother in arms, and I respected him. It was no surprise, then, that Shep would be generous with his house when I was in need.

Determinedly, Shep and I made a plan and executed it. When I gathered my belongings, the only conversation I had with my parents was about what I could and could not take. I could take the used daybed set a friend had passed down to me years before, but the dresser stayed. I packed my clothes and some small personal items in boxes and headed for the door. Mom and Dad did not seem concerned that I was moving out as a minor while still in high school. They didn't offer to help in any way. They didn't say goodbye. As I left, closing the front door behind me, I realized that a part of my life was over.

My parents weren't the only ones unconcerned with two teenaged boys living on their own; *no one* seemed to care. Naturally, that served me just fine. I was free from the constant barrage of negativity, manipulation, and loneliness.

For years, I'd had seasonal jobs working construction. I had started learning the trade from one of my scoutmasters, Drew. He and I had an agreement: when I was fourteen, I worked for him free, providing manual labor to help him build his house. In exchange, he taught me how to build. I worked construction off and on for nearly three years on weekends, holidays, and during summers. When I graduated from high school, Drew hired me full time. Shep and I thought we were hot shit. Living on our own and working together doing construction, we had it pretty good.

One night, the doorbell rang at Shep's house. Shelly, Shep's sister, answered it and announced that Troy was there.

"Hey, Troy," I greeted him, puzzled.

Troy was my nephew, my older sister Karen's son. He was actually seven months older than me, making me an uncle before I was born. I grew up with Troy, his younger brother Trevor, and sister Tisha, living together for a few years when Karen moved back to my parents' house after her divorce. However, Troy and I were never particularly close. After all, he was masculine, confident, and athletic. Now that we were older, though, I did see him twice a week at the youth ministry that he, Trevor, and I attended.

"What's going on?" I asked him.

"You know Markam went into the Marines?" Troy asked. Markam

was Troy's good friend from high school whom I had met a few times. "And he loves it!" Troy continued. "I'm thinking about it, too. I wanted to see if you would come with me."

I blinked. Marine Corps? Me?

"They have a buddy program that lets us enlist together and go to boot camp in the same platoon," Troy said, filling my silence.

I was waiting for the punch line. Seriously, Troy did not need me to do this. Besides, what did he see in me that made him think I'd be a good choice? I don't know if I was in shock or just relishing that Troy, who always seemed so confident, seemed to need me in order for him to make his move, but I heard myself say, "Okay."

So it was with that little conversation and only slightly more thought that my future was altered. We agreed to go to the recruiters together and check it out, but in my mind, I was already committed.

Up until that time, I hadn't considered what I wanted to do next. It wasn't until I was offered an option that I even recognized the lack of direction of my current state. As a child, I was never challenged to think about my future. No one asked me, "What's your dream?" Today, this is one of my first questions I ask young people. I know that children do not dream of failing, and need someone to hear what they do dream of. We need to get them thinking of the next chapters in their lives in advance. Like any journey we take in life, the first thing we need to know is where we want to go. In many of the families I have worked with, the parent has no clue what his or her child dreams of becoming. If we don't ask, we are missing one of the biggest conversations we can have with our children. By supporting a child's dreams, parenting becomes much easier. And the future seems much brighter to the child.

I had just turned eighteen by the time Troy and I signed our papers on November 2, 1982. Under a delayed entry program, we were scheduled to begin boot camp in January 1983 in San Diego.

Going into the military was seductive. I'd played with toy soldiers when I was a kid and was mesmerized by Army movies. My grandfather was a World War I Navy vet, my dad was a World War II Army vet, and my brother was a Vietnam Navy vet, so the military was not a foreign concept. Of course, as soon as I signed the papers, all the doubts crept in. What if I couldn't do it? What if I couldn't make it? What if I proved my father right—that I was stupid and would never amount to anything? Who was I to think I could actually become a *Marine*, the best of the military? However, it was too late to turn back. The contract was signed. My fate was sealed.

With these fears, I embarked on sixteen weeks of training. The first big shocker came the night our bus stopped alongside an old yellowish stucco building at the Marine Corps Recruit Depot in San Diego. A Marine boarded the bus and barked orders, and then yelled, "You have thirty seconds to get off my bus! Move! Move! Move!" All of us recruits scurried off the bus, where we ran into another Marine redirecting our route at the top of his lungs. We ran to what looked like a garden shed. Once there, another Marine yelled for us to grab green canvas bags, which I soon learned were called "sea bags." We each hauled one and ran back toward the building. My heart was pounding so hard it felt like it was going to punch a hole in my chest. As I approached the building, several Marines yelled at us as they lined us up in rows on painted yellow footprints. These footprints, I discovered, are where recruits first learn to stand at the position of attention. If you were not scared shitless when you first got off the bus, you sure as hell were by now. These men were larger than life. Their uniforms were impeccable. Their demeanor was terrifying. I was so scared that I was afraid to move a muscle, and I stood motionless on a set of footprints, trying to figure out what was being asked of me.

That first night was rough. As we finally hit the racks and turned the lights off sometime around two in the morning, I remember hearing other boys crying. Why were they crying? I wondered. Hadn't anyone ever yelled at them? For me, the fear came from not knowing what was coming next. As long as someone gave direction, I could cope with the request, but the constant wondering of what the hell was coming was unnerving.

This first part of the journey was called "receiving." It wasn't so bad. We went to the joint receiving barracks to wait for additional recruits to arrive from other parts of the country; together, we would become the Third Training Battalion. While we waited, we had a "troop handler," who was like a drill instructor on "vacation." He was firm but not fearsome, and I remember feeling reassured. *Yeah. I can do this.*

After two weeks of basic paperwork, additional testing, and equipment issue, we were ready for the real training with the real drill instructors. One night, the troop handler introduced us to our drill instructors. Holy shit! These guys were mean, mean, mean! Drill Instructor Sergeant Ostoy had been a force reconnaissance Marine in Vietnam. He'd gone deep behind enemy lines—one hundred *miles* across the dangerous other side. He was amazing—built like a fire-plug, short and stout, with a chiseled face that never smiled. Senior Drill Instructor Staff Sergeant Carter was an international chaser— literally. He went around the world and chased people the government wanted. He was lean and mean and had a crooked index finger on his right hand, which I saw a lot of and always wondered how that finger became so disjointed. Drill Instructor Staff Sergeant Bias was just mean all the time, but to hear his left-right-left cadence to the rhythm of the "Marines' Hymn" was truly inspiring, and he only did it when he was proud of us for doing something well. When he called his cadence, our chests puffed out that much more, and our heels struck the deck with a crisp whack. All of the drill instructors (DIs) were total bad asses and scary as hell. My number one defense mechanism, humor, was not going to work here—it was not even an option! And there was no escape from the fear—no place to take a time-out or catch a break. It was unrelenting. I had to deal with the fear, become bedfellows with it. So I went to sleep scared and woke up with a DI screaming, "Move, move, move!" I started each day fighting my fears.

The whole premise of boot camp is to break recruits down physically and mentally to rebuild and shape them into warriors. Recruits are yelled at constantly and for the smallest infraction. They are verbally "tuned up." There was a time when DIs could hit recruits, but I had come into the Marine Corps just as they were phasing out that practice. Instead of beatings, they exerted us physically until we were completely exhausted. Every moment was regulated. We had to get permission to take a piss. From the moment I woke up to the moment I went to bed, I was terrified of saying or doing the wrong thing. I was terrified of looking one of these men in the eye, of forgetting the equipment I needed, of not knowing what I was doing and incurring their wrath. I stood at attention while large men hollered in my face, trying not to let them see how real my fear was. No recruit enjoyed that treatment, but some took it better than others. It made me freeze in my tracks. I was the proverbial deer in the headlights and couldn't do anything about it. Maybe that intimidation sprung from the deep-seated fear I had as a child when my mother shook me and yelled in my face, but whatever the reason, it made my survival of boot camp questionable. Rejection was commonplace, and humiliation was the norm.

"Hey, Mark, you've got to pick it up." Troy pulled me aside as we walked through the squad bay in that first month of boot camp.

"What do you mean?" I asked, glancing around to make sure no DIs were nearby.

"I put entries in the record book," Troy reminded me. Naturally, Troy had not only acclimated quickly, but the DIs had asked him to be the platoon scribe and take on some administrative tasks. One of the things he did was write entries into the recruit files.

"They say you're insecure and immature," he said. "They say you most likely won't make it through boot camp. So if you want to make it, you have to do something."

Hurt and embarrassed, I turned and walked away. Troy had good intentions, but I already knew I was struggling and overwhelmed. Now, to get definitive proof, and for that proof to come from my older nephew . . . a deep anger grew with me. It wasn't the fire-hot anger of out-of-control emotion, but a smoldering, long-lasting fury that stoked my determination: the drill instructors were not going to kick me out. I was going to succeed, no matter what. It had taken over eight weeks for me to choose to turn *toward* my fears instead of away from them, but I was tired of running away inside.

It was time for me to grow up and become a man. To do that, I also had to choose which message the adults in my life had spoken the loudest: my parents' belief that I was a failure, deserving of rejection, or my sister's, troop leaders', and friends' belief that I was skilled, worthy, and helpful. I chose to listen to the love spoken into my life.

It was not long after that conversation with Troy that I was assigned to the position of Head Pisser Private. That meant I was now in charge of cleaning the urinals, the toilets, the showers, and the sinks. For whatever reason I was chosen, I knew that I was going to own the cleanest of bathrooms. That would not be an easy task. About one hundred recruits used this massive bathroom, and everything was tile except the fixtures, which were metal. Every fixture had to be so clean you could see your reflection, with no water spots whatsoever. The drains in the tile floor were made of brass, and that brass had to shine. Ten recruits cleaned the head with me, and because we were given a short period of time to clean all of the facilities, we had to work together with clear direction to accomplish the task. Just like when I was a Scout leader with my group of rebels, we excelled at our tasks, keeping everything spotlessly clean and smelling Pine-Sol fresh.

Shortly after I became Head Pisser Private, Drill Instructor Sergeant Ostoy emerged from the duty hut and stood in front of the platoon. We were all sitting in the classroom cleaning our weapons when he announced that he needed a lay leader to assist the chaplain.

Sergeant Ostoy never talked much, so when he did, you listened. He took a moment and looked each of us in the eye.

"If anyone thinks Christians are weak, you're wrong," he said. "I am a Christian, and if you think I am weak, let's step outside."

The room was silent. Satisfied, he went on.

"How many of you are Christians?" he barked.

Several of us timidly raised our hands. He looked around and his eyes settled on me.

"Cripe," he pointed. "You are the platoon's Protestant lay leader."

That sounded good to me. I had grown up in a non-denominational church and started helping out in a youth ministry with Troy right before I enlisted. This seemed like something I could do.

Every Sunday, the entire platoon was allowed to sleep in until six in the morning. We then went to chow and to the mandatory church services of our choice. All of us went to a church service, but we were allowed to choose which religious service to attend. No one was allowed to stay behind in the barracks on Sunday morning. After morning services, lay leaders would spend time with the chaplains of their religion. Since I was Platoon 3009's Protestant lay leader, I got to spend time with the Protestant chaplain. He was a Marine Corps colonel but unlike any other Marine I had encountered. An older man with thin silver hair, he was full of compassion. He spoke gently, with comforting, encouraging words. He taught the other lay leaders and me how to assist in giving last rites, set up the mobile altar, prepare for communion, and perform all of the services Marines do in the field, because if we were deployed, we would assist that field chaplain. For me, the most important lesson he taught was how powerful a tenderly spoken word was and how it could positively impact a young life. Clear direction doesn't have to be shouted; it can come from a calm and compassionate place.

Even though I was starting to improve my game, I was often still scared. Every time I passed another platoon's drill instructor (or worse, an officer), I felt like I would shit a brick. That insecure, self-doubting fear made conscious thought impossible. But if I messed up my greeting—stopping and coming to attention until a drill instructor said, "By your leave"—all hell broke loose: the DI would yell at me about how I'd screwed up, while the only thing I could think was, *I was just trying to get back to my platoon!* Then I would have to wait for my DIs to be "advised" of what had happened and suffer whatever wrath they cooked up.

During boot camp, our platoon went to Camp Pendleton, near Oceanside, California, for rifle qualification and recruit field training. This was when the DIs marched us into the ground. We arrived on a bus, and our large olive drab canvas sea bags used to carry everything we owned arrived after us on a truck. When that truck arrived, everyone rushed to grab a sea bag, regardless of whether or not it belonged to him, because a drill instructor was, of course, yelling at us to grab a bag and go. But now everyone had someone else's gear and didn't know who it belonged to or how to get it back to him. I surveyed the disorganized, chaotic situation and sighed, realizing that I was making a decision to try to lead.

"Sir! Recruit Cripe requesting permission to speak, sir!" I said outside, properly not looking at the nearest drill instructor.

"Cripe! Get in the pit!" ordered the DI. The pit was a big sand/mud pit, where we went to do pushups. By the time I was done with my forty-five minutes of "thrashing," my uniform was solid mud. In fact, the tee shirt and boxers I wore under my uniform that day never lost the tan color from the mud stains.

"What do you want, Cripe?" the DI asked when I finished. I explained that everyone's bags were mixed up and requested permission to remedy it.

"Get in there and square it away," he ordered.

"Yes, sir!" I said and went inside. "Okay, guys, let's get this straight," I said, and we sorted the whole thing out by calling out the name on the sea bag we were holding. Eventually every sea bag found its way to the correct recruit. By the time the DI ordered us to stow our "shit" in our foot lockers, we each had our own bag and could organize our foot lockers right the first time. Early on in boot camp, the DIs spent four hours teaching us exactly how they wanted the footlockers to be. Every item had its special place, so when any recruit's footlocker was opened, it looked exactly like the others. I thought for sure that my sacrifice for the platoon had gone unnoticed. No one said thank you, but I knew each recruit realized that the sea bags were all mixed up but allowed fear to paralyze them into non-action. I was just the first recruit to conquer his fear at that moment and actually do something about it.

That night, DI Staff Sergeant Carter yelled "Recruit Cripe!" from the duty hut. The duty hut was where the DIs lived while on duty, and it was never a good thing to be called in there. For recruits, this summons usually ended up with them being fired. One recruit was even arrested. I hustled over there, fear welling up inside. I was getting kicked out—or worse, I would have to start boot camp over. I racked my brain, trying to think of what I had done that was bad enough to warrant a trip inside the hut from hell, but my mental search turned up empty.

At the hut, I pounded hard on the wall three times, just as we were trained to do. "Recruit Cripe reporting as requested, sir!" I called.

"Get your ass in here," Staff Sergeant Carter commanded.

It took everything I had to find the center of the desk and stand just the right distance away. I stood front and center, at attention, waiting for the ax to fall. Already, I hated every second of this experience. I couldn't see the DI's expression because I wasn't supposed to look him in the eye. He talked, and I braced myself for a harsh tone, but I could barely hear his words for the pounding of my heart as I waited for him to get to the bottom line.

"You've really turned yourself around, Cripe," he said.

Wait. Did he just say . . . ?

"I am extremely impressed with you and want you to be my fourth squad leader."

Shocked, I managed, "Yes, sir!"

Then there was an awkward moment in which I had no idea what to do next.

Staff Sergeant Carter finally broke the silence. Without looking up at me as he continued to do some paperwork, he firmly stated, "Well, get the hell out of here!"

"Sir. Yes, sir. Thank you, sir!" I stammered as I took a clumsy step back and about-faced to exit the room "quickly and smartly." I finally let out the breath I had been holding. Staff Sergeant Carter was impressed? I couldn't believe it. I had gone from a terrified recruit to Head Pisser Private, to lay leader to the fourth squad leader. As squad leader, I would supervise about twenty recruits, and I knew that if I retained that spot throughout boot camp, I would get a meritorious promotion at the end. Somehow, I was finding my way. I was defining who I was and who I would become.

The difference between my first weeks as a recruit and later, when I was just as scared but able to perform and react, was something I had learned and made my mantra: "Slow is smooth, smooth is fast." The faster I tried to do something, the more my fingers fumbled, the more my tongue tripped over itself, and the more my thoughts scrambled. Think about opening a combination lock in ten seconds. If you try to rush with a guy yelling at you, you're going to have to twist that combination three or four times before the lock clicks open. But if you intentionally slow down and turn that dial deliberately, you end up opening the lock a lot faster. I focused on the idea that slow is fast, slowing my mind down so I could actually think and move more deliberately, concentrating on getting that one thing right. That helped me calm down in moments of fear or doubt, and it's what I do today. When I get into a state of crisis, I break it down to what my immediate next step should be and I proceed that way. What are the most basic steps that I need to do to achieve the goal? Opening a combination lock was broken down into several small steps. First, focus on the dial, shutting out all the other distractions. Second, slowly turn the dial to the right until the first number of the combination aligns with the little white line on the top. Third, stop and breathe, then fourth, slowly turn the dial to the left until the next number aligns. Stop, breathe, and so on. Those baby steps that guided me through boot camp have continued to serve me well.

As intimidated as I was by the DIs, one in particular taught me a vital lesson. We were in the field at Camp Pendleton and had been issued MREs (Meal, Ready to Eat). Somehow, one of the recruits in my squad lost his MRE. How you lose your meal, I don't know, but the DI noticed.

"One of your men doesn't have an MRE, Cripe," he barked.

"Yes, sir," I responded.

He looked at me expectantly. "What are you going to do about it?"

Shit! I was hungry. "I'm going to give him mine, sir," I said.

He nodded. "Exactly right. That's what a leader does."

I went over there and gave the scrub my MRE, my eyes conveying my displeasure. Then I went back to my spot and sat down with no chow. Leadership sucked. But he was right. Leadership has two parts to it. One is knowing what to do, and the other is actually doing it. Without saying a word, the DI came back over and handed me his MRE.

Now, maybe he had access to a whole truck full of MREs, but it didn't matter. I was amazed that he would give up his meal for me, even though he'd just told me to do the same thing for the recruit. It was the first time a grown man had sacrificed to make sure my needs were met. He modeled a very powerful lesson—as a leader, he would not ask me to do something he wouldn't do himself.

• • •

I survived boot camp. I remained fourth squad leader throughout and meritoriously promoted at the end. As graduation day came, we retired the title of *recruit* and were awarded the title that less than one percent of Americans earn: United States Marine, a title I will wear proudly forever.

That day was about celebrating accomplishments. My emotions ran high as friends and family came to see the Third Battalion march out onto that parade deck—a pageant of boys who had been turned into Marines who were ready to defend our country, our Constitution, and our way of life. The words "land of the free and home of the brave" took on a whole new meaning for me, and I was proud of everything American.

After graduation, as my parents and I walked across the parade deck area, my father looked around at all the grandeur of the Marine Corps Recruit Depot. There are only two places in the world where Marines are made. One is Parris Island, South Carolina, and the other is in San Diego. This place was hallowed ground for Marines. Living history stands everywhere you look. From the yellow footprints of the receiving barracks to the chow hall to the massive three story barracks, men who had fought in some of our most courageous battles and whose names were recorded in history had walked before us. Red and yellow signs boldly announced every building. A huge garrison flag was raised and lowered every day to the sound of reveille and taps. Marines strutted everywhere, impressing onlookers with dress blues and alpha uniforms. This place screamed confidence through superior leadership.

"I would have gone into the Marines if I thought I could have done it," my father said.

I slowly turned my head toward him, but he didn't meet my gaze. I realized that my father was actually paying me a compliment—the first one he'd ever given me. I felt a sense of contentment but didn't say anything in return. I just kept walking, knowing inside that I had become more than this man next to me. Honor, courage, and commitment would prevail from that point on.

I love YOU.
I want YOU.
I need YOU.

A CALL TO LEAD ERSHIP

CHAPTER 4

THE CAMPFIRE SCENE LOOKED LIKE SOMETHING FROM A MOVIE: the fire crackling in the pit along the forested shores of Hamilton Lake and the massive granite peaks of the High Sierras cutting into the star-filled night sky. The eleven members of our wilderness group looked at one another uncertainly. The youngest was thirteen, and the oldest was twenty-three, but most were college-aged students, both males and females. All were new to the backcountry, but they were here acquiring the skills that would prepare them for an upcoming missions trip to Mexico. In twelve days, covering one hundred and ten miles, including scaling three fourteen-thousand-foot peaks, they would learn about the struggles of backpacking in the Sierras. More importantly, they would learn how to function as a cohesive team.

At the time, I had been working as a wilderness leader for several years. Sometimes I facilitated trips like this for church groups of adults or teens. Often it was for CEOs and the top executives in their business. But I was new to this wilderness company, Sea and Summit Expeditions. This was my first trip with that company.

On our second day, I pulled the senior leader, Gail, aside and asked her if we could try a team-building activity I had devised. Gail looked at me, considering. In her late twenties with her brunette hair clasped back in a swinging ponytail, Gail could almost be mistaken for one of the college kids in the group. But her low-key approach and endless energy spoke of her confidence and experience. In fact, this was one of Gail's last tours as a wilderness instructor. She was ready to move on to new adventures, but she was still willing to work with a newbie like me.

At the beginning of our trip, Gail and I started a unique practice; we would walk some distance away from the group and then stop to observe them. We took turns verbalizing what we saw our team doing. Amazingly, as I heard myself describe what I was seeing, I somehow saw more. "Laura is sitting on the rock by herself," for example, might be a casual observation, but it caused us to pay attention to Laura. Was she sitting apart from the group? Was she enjoying solitary time? Was she upset? Did she frequently separate herself from the others? These observations caused us to think about what our eyes were actually seeing and to be more aware of the needs of the individuals and of the group. It was during one of these moments when Gail said that she thought we should try my new initiative. We talked about what and how we would facilitate this new activity.

One thing that divides people—makes it harder for them to trust each other—is the fear of what others are thinking. We all worry that the other people in our group think as negatively of us as we do of ourselves, so our defenses are up even before anything happens. What if, instead of having those thoughts and doubts go round and round in our heads, we shared them with the group and the group, in turn, shared its perceptions of us? I believed that once each person shared his or her thoughts and worries about the group's perception, the group would provide unequivocal support, rewarding the person's willingness to be vulnerable with empathy and confirmation.

Now, however, as the group huddled around the campfire, I hesitated, wondering if it was a good idea. Suppose I was wrong and this activity turned negative? It could damage the individuals, sabotage the entire group dynamic, and certainly make this my first and last wilderness expedition with this company. But my gut said it would work, so I sat down on a log near the group and explained that the activity involved trust and vulnerability. I explained the goal and the steps and allowed them to ask any questions they had. I also gave them an out: they could decline if the risk was too high—after all, I didn't want to encourage rejection. We were treading in dangerous waters and I needed to be on the top of my game to protect the dignity of each team member. I relaxed my body so I could be at ease and still, focusing on every word spoken.

"Would someone like to volunteer to start?" I asked. For a moment, the night sounds of the forest could be heard over the popping sounds of the fire. Then a soft timid voice emerged.

"I'll go," said Justin, the thirteen-year-old who had already been in California Youth Authority, a large youth correctional system. Justin was a product of the foster care system, and he was starving for something . . . more. Just the day before, the first day of the trip, Justin had stopped and dropped his pack in the middle of the trail.

"I quit!" he announced.

I could have told him that he was stuck with us and that there was no going back so he had to go forward. Or, as a last resort, we could have called for a rescue, but Justin wasn't hurt or sick. He was just suddenly scared that he couldn't do the trip. So, like a parent who allows squabbling siblings to work out a problem, I turned the issue over to the group and sat down on the hillside, leaning on my backpack. For me, it was a great opportunity to model lessons I had learned. I had found a calm and compassionate place within myself where I could empathize with Justin but not enable him. Soon, as the group realized I was not getting mad and was not going to force the moment, they began to positively react to Justin. Rejection was not going to be spoken here!

"Come on, Justin. Let me help you," said Carrie, as she walked over to Justin and opened his backpack. "Why don't I carry something to make your backpack lighter? That will make it easier, right?" she asked with an encouraging smile.

With that, other people in the group surrounded Justin, splitting up his gear to lighten his burden.

"You can do it, man," said Keith, one of the oldest in the group.

I hid my smile of satisfaction. The group, on its own, had encouraged Justin and gotten him to recommit to finishing the journey.

After walking another mile unburdened, Justin stopped again.

"I'll take my gear back now," he said, and after he re-packed his backpack, he never looked back.

Now, at the fireside, he was taking another big step. He was choosing to lead his group into unknown territory and become completely vulnerable.

"My mom was a crack addict, and I never knew my dad. I don't even know if my mom knew my dad," he began. "She gave me up when I was seven, said I was too much work, with social services always coming around to find out why I wasn't in school, or when I was, why I had bruises and stuff."

This young man knew rejection well; his self-concept was hard for me to hear without getting up and giving him a big hug. He continued to share, and right in front of our eyes, he went from a hard-ass little boy to a scared child hiding from further rejection.

"Nobody wants a kid like me," he continued. "I'm too old to be cute. Foster families think I'm going to steal from them or do crack like my mom. There's no place for me. I'm just waiting until I turn eighteen and then—and then, I don't know. But I heard about this trip, see, and I thought it might get me away from being *me* for awhile."

His negative attitude on the trail the day before now made sense. His eyes focused on the ground as he finished. Now, for the scary part—it was the group's turn to share how they saw Justin.

"Justin, man, you're very brave," said Keith.

Justin shrugged.

"No, really," Keith insisted. "It's incredible that you have taken on this goal, without anyone's support."

"Only a strong person could do that," Laura added.

Others in the group nodded in agreement as Justin looked up warily. The power of affirmation is an amazing thing. I watched the faces and listened to every word as the group embraced Justin with positive and encouraging comments. They built a whole new paradigm for Justin. In addition to *brave*, they used words like courageous, kind, and giving to describe how they saw a scared child who had embarked on a life-changing journey.

I looked across the blazing campfire at Gail and grinned. This was exactly the reaction I had hoped to see. The group had to become vulnerable with each other and begin shedding their self-doubt in order to become stronger as individuals and as a team. It was an emotionally risky exercise, since most of the team had only met recently, but I felt sure that doing it this early would help the group bond faster and tighter than anything else. The group could have been critical or reluctant to embrace the exercise, but instead, they cooperated and let their guard down in an amazingly effective way.

It wasn't the same as boot camp, but it was a method of getting a disparate group to put aside misconceptions and fear and learn instead to rely on each other, to be courageously vulnerable, and to be big enough to make someone else matter. Nothing brings people closer than feeling that they must work together for survival. And out here, in the wilderness, that was completely true.

Gail and I were leading this group mostly off-trail, which is not as safe as being on the trail, but it would more closely mimic what the group would experience in Mexico. Our off-trail route would lead us up the Mountaineers Route of Mount Whitney's north face, which had a summit of 14,505 feet, the highest summit in the contiguous United States. Even though this was August, at its peak, Mount Whitney's north face could be covered in ice. With dangers from the elements, the environment, and the natural wildlife to cope with, trekking it provided essential lessons on trust born from vulnerability and teamwork—the same lessons I had learned during those terrifying weeks of boot camp.

• • •

When boot camp ended, I had gone to Infantry Training School on Camp Pendleton and then on to my Reserve Unit; Delta Company, Second Battalion Twenty-Third Marine Regiment, Fourth Marine

Division. I had enlisted on a six-year contract that required one weekend a month and at least a two-week annual training deployment—that is, if our country did not go to war, at which time I could be activated for full-time service. I had no idea of all the changes that would occur in those six years. As I settled back into civilian life, I enrolled in community college, majoring in psychology with a minor in sociology, while also working my way up the ladder in United Parcel Service. A year and half later, I transferred to Biola University, a small Christian college in La Mirada, California.

The decision to go to Biola was based on my desire to become a youth pastor—but it was also heavily influenced by a girl I began dating right before I enlisted, and who became my fiancé. She was in college and encouraged me to go into a four-year school, too. However, our engagement ended abruptly when she decided to move to Oregon for medical school. Although this was probably the right decision for her, I wasn't ready to move again and decided not to follow her. Even though that decision was mine, I still felt hurt and rejected. Once again, the wilderness became my solace, and I escaped my emotional upheaval by rock climbing.

I quickly discovered that my Reserve check wasn't enough to cover living expenses. I picked up work at Sir Speedy Printing and was hired by Disneyland as a professional rock climber, scaling and rappelling the Matterhorn, a popular bobsled ride at the park. I also earned a scholarship from Biola by building stages for their drama department.

After taking several upper level psych classes, I realized that I did not want to be a psychologist. Education seemed a more practical major, and with a minor in camp and recreation, it was a natural combination. Ever since I was a leader in Scouts, I had gravitated to the idea of helping people accomplish their goals by teaching them skills so they could succeed. The idea of doing all of that through experiential education in the wilderness—well, that was the ultimate combination.

Will Toms was a guest lecturer in one of my college classes. He and his wife, Millie, operated Sea and Summit Expeditions, a ministry that helped youth and adults with a variety of challenges. Will is known as one of the "grandfathers" of California backcountry adventure programming. Tim and Bob—my college climbing buddies—and I thought that Will was a genuine role model because he was doing what we were only dreaming of doing. The three of us had arranged an outing with Will one night just to spend time with a legend in the field we wanted to get into. While we drove to an adventure presentation in Fullerton, Will started a conversation.

"What's important to you?" he asked. "What are your three greatest loves and your three greatest fears?"

Tim, Bob, and I looked at each other questioningly but answered the best we could. My loves were easy: God, my country, and my family. (Yes, I took the easy ones.) But the fears were hard to answer. I started with the fear of failing and struggled with the other two. After all, no one had ever asked me what I feared. I did not even know what I was worried about failing. I only knew that life seemed so big and I felt so small. I never did finish that answer for Will. However, it echoes in my head even today. What did I fear? And what did I really love? The answer is constantly evolving.

Another time, Will asked me, "What makes you so confident?" I was confused by his question. I certainly never felt that confident. I marveled at how someone's perception of me could be so far from my perception of myself and what that meant for the way I saw others. Just by asking questions, Will planted seeds in my mind that would play out significantly in my future.

Even though my buddies and I were hoping to work for him that summer, we didn't get hired, and I didn't see Will for several years. In the meantime, even while I was leading small local wilderness expeditions, I still hiked and climbed regularly with a group of my friends. One day, on a whim, Dave, Tim, Bob, and I decided to go rock climbing at a formation fondly known as Trash Can Rock in Joshua Tree National Monument. We were poor college kids, and one of the guys forgot his beat-up climbing shoes. So as I topped the short route out, I took off my shoes and threw them down so he could put them on to climb up. While I waited for him, I decided to hop along the top of the rock and talk with Dave. As I rounded the corner of a large boulder, I saw Dave trying to belay Tim while talking to a girl and helping her with something on her harness. As Dave saw me, he asked if I could help her because she was bugging him in his belaying duties. I laughed and said I'd help. This girl had forgotten to bring her rappel device up with her, so I set up a "biner brake" with her carabiners so she could safely rappel down the rock. She looked up and to thank me, and I was smitten with her big smile and laughing brown eyes immediately. The guys instantly saw that I liked her, and when she asked for my phone number, I thought they were going to faint with excitement. Her name was Melanie, and we climbed together as friends for a long time after that. She had a spirit of adventure and enjoyed climbing and camping, yet she helped keep me grounded.

When we look back, it's amazing that we even met. Both her friends and mine were at that location by chance. Had either of us gone earlier or later, our futures might have never intertwined. It was predestined, she says. She wanted me to kiss her long before I did, and I had no idea at the time, because I certainly would have accommodated her.

Melanie was a nurse and four months older than me. Her family was better off than mine, which wasn't hard, and they were close. Her father died when she was six years old, and as we got to know each other, I realized that she had deep-seated insecurities, just like me. These hidden insecurities played out in conflicts between the two of us, testing our commitment to each other. The youthfulness of our love kept us together in the early years, but as we matured, we learned how to say, "I love you, I want you, I need you" more often and more tenderly. The more time we spent together, I realized that Mel, as I called her, was "the one." We married and continued to share our passion for adventure.

• • •

I ran into Will Toms again at a wilderness leaders consortium meeting in Oregon two years later.

Will asked about my experiences since the last time we met, and I told him I had been running small wilderness trips for churches, but nothing big. I had, however, become a climbing nut, living and breathing anything climbing related.

"I'm looking for an instructor for a summer trip—a trans-Sierra trip," he said.

Right up my alley, I thought, and told him I would be happy to apply. He must have thought that was a good thing. The ease I felt in the wilderness may have appeared to be cockiness to others, but having spent so much of my life feeling insecure, the idea of being overly confident was amusing.

Just as my Scout leaders had taught me how to lead others in my troop, Will Toms taught me how to lead others in the wilderness. Lean, with a long face and stern blue eyes but a firm, fair manner, Will took me under his wing. He hired me even though I was young for a wilderness instructor.

Will used an exercise when he worked with a group going on an expedition to set the stage for success. He did what he called a five-finger contract to teach the group what was important. The thumb is a reminder to keep it positive: thumbs up. The index or pointing finger reminds us not to blame. The middle finger says not to swear. The ring finger is a symbol of commitment, and the baby finger or pinky is about supporting the weakest person in the group. Every time Will went on a trip, he had the group commit to the trip and to the contract.

Expeditions like this can be scary for new hikers. Many of them are testing themselves, their character, in all ways possible. The hikes are physically demanding with long, exhausting days of climbing. New hikers wonder if they can make it. But there's no other option. There's no backing out once the expedition has started. They can't call for a cab or ask a friend to pick them up. They have to keep going even when their backpacks rub raw spots along their shoulders or hip, even when blisters form on their feet and burst in their boots days later, and even when every muscle aches from days of sleeping on the ground and their heads pound from trudging in the sun. Not only do they have to keep going, the rest of the team needs to *know* that everyone will keep going. Once the hike is over and the team members recognize what they have actually done, everyone feels a phenomenal sense of accomplishment that carries over in all aspects of their lives. They have an internal affirmation that they matter, which helps silence all the negative voices they have heard over the years. Wilderness leaders understand the end game. But we also recognize that new hikers haven't seen the finish line yet, so we need to give them that confidence, that sense of commitment, to keep them going when they let fear consume them and they doubt their ability.

In the Marine Corps, when I was terrified during those first weeks of boot camp, I coped by slowing down, focusing on each task to get it done right. That's one strategy I used when facilitating groups on wilderness treks. As scary as it was for the hikers to take on this big adventure, I felt an enormous responsibility to make sure they were safe.

On my first hike with Will's company, with Gail and Justin and all the others in our small group, I didn't want to mess up. And I didn't. Not everything went perfectly, but everyone emerged from the trek safe and well. In fact, when the trip was over, Will pulled me aside.

"Mark, I'm very impressed with what you did," he said. "And I apologize for not hiring you two years ago when we first met."

Will's commendation and support meant the world to me. Just as I wanted to please my Scout leaders, I wanted to please him, and hearing his praise helped soothe a place in me that still needed parental approval, even at the age of twenty-three. Since I was a Scout, I knew I was good at navigating the wilderness. But Will's confidence in me added something else I was gifted at: facilitating people. The idea of doing more of it filled me with anticipation. It was addictive. To help facilitate a human experience that significantly changes the way someone thinks is an awesome responsibility that brings tremendous joy to me, and I knew I wanted to do that more.

• • •

Mel and I took our next big adventure by backpacking through thirteen countries in Europe for four months. Before our trip, we sold practically all of our belongings, and we knew that we would have to rebuild our lives when we came back.

"I've got a place you can stay when you get back," said Steve, a buddy of mine. "I've got some property I am going to build a house on some day—you could live in a tent there. You can stay there rent-free."

Then Steve's free-spirited side came out. "You know what? Forget the tent. How about a teepee?"

Mel and I were used to camping, so a teepee it was. We set it all up before we left, even living in it for a couple of months before our trip to save more money. When we left, we went on one of the greatest adventures of our lives, but not one without defining moments.

One of those moments came to Mel and me in a little German town called Freiburg. The day before, we had gotten into an argument about something neither of us can remember now. We were sitting in a train station in Barcelona when the argument started. As we hissed and bickered at each other, Mel wriggled her wedding ring off her finger.

"I don't want it anymore," she said primly as she handed it to me. I snatched it and put it in my pocket. But as angry as we were, we never left the other's side, boarding our train north to Germany pissed off at each other. The ride lasted through the night, and when Mel cooled off, she wanted her ring back. But I wasn't over my mad yet, and I refused to give it to her. As the train slowed at the Freiburg stop, we decided to get off. I walked to the doorway and climbed down the steps of the train, but when I stepped on the platform, Mel was not behind me, and the train had to leave. I quickly climbed back aboard, only to see Mel at the other end of the train car in a panic, trying to get off to get to platform where she thought I was. But other passengers had blocked her path. As the train began chugging, Mel pulled the emergency cord, and the train screeched to a stop.

Apparently, in Germany, it was a crime to use that cord unless there was a real emergency, so we were escorted off the train by armed police officers.

After paying a fine and being released, Mel and I looked sheepishly at each other. We had both been childish. After all, neither one of us wanted to be apart from the other, but instead, we escalated the argument like a poker game. We wanted to force each other to admit that the other mattered, but we were doing it from a place of fear, which ultimately only caused more fear.

"Let's not do that again," Mel said, and I nodded. We made a pact. Instead, we promised to simply say, "I love you, I want you, I need you." We voided the word "divorce" from our vocabulary and committed to not quitting. Sure, that's what our wedding vows were about, but still, defining moments tested the meaning of those vows.

When we got back to teepee, sweet teepee, it certainly challenged us to maintain our now weathered newlywed bliss. Even though it was large, about twenty feet wide, it had no running water or electricity. In effect, we were homeless, camping in the desert.

Eventually, we found a four-hundred-square-foot remodeled garage to call home and began to settle down like responsible grown-ups. We still led wilderness expeditions on a volunteer basis and rocked climbed whenever possible, and we were on the threshold of making some very important changes.

~~ANGER~~
~~FRUSTRATION~~
fear.

NO SECOND
CHANCE

CHAPTER 5

THAT FIRST DAY ON PATROL, AS OUR BLACK AND WHITE PULLED UP NEAR
THE DRIVEWAY OF THE YELLOW STUCCO HOME, I HAD NO IDEA OF THE CRISIS
I WOULD FACE OR THE INDELIBLE IMPACT IT WOULD HAVE ON ME.

I had worked in the custody division of the L.A. County Sheriff's
Department for six and a half years, ever since realizing—at the ripe
old age of twenty-six—that I needed to grow up. Melanie was pregnant, and it was obvious that I needed to bring in a paycheck from
a steady job every week. I loved being a wilderness instructor, but I
needed to find a new job. I'd first applied for a facility maintenance
job with the county but was turned down because I did not have
enough plumbing experience. Then one day, as I was driving into
town in my old beat-up Ford truck, I passed the county jail. Standing just beyond the gates, I saw a chubby deputy with a cowboy hat
drinking a steaming cup of hot coffee as he watched the inmates work.

I could do that job, I thought. I had never particularly wanted
to be in law enforcement. Most of the cops I had run into had not
been kind. But I was desperate, and I knew I could stand around
and watch inmates work. Little did I know that that was not the job
but merely one of many assignments.

I drove to the sheriff's station and asked the secretary about
the application process. To my surprise, I found out I needed less
experience for a deputy position than I did for a maintenance position, yet I'd be paid more. I took the application but still wasn't sure.
A deputy? Me? I kept looking at jobs available and realized that with
any job, I would have to start at the bottom rung. I was currently

working at a fast food joint called In-N-Out Burger, but I had to make more money for our new baby. So I continued the application process for the sheriff's department. After about eight months, I got the phone call telling me that I was hired. Even though I was grateful for the income and benefits, I immediately wondered if I had made a mistake. This was so different from the wilderness leadership I had done, where I was helping people test and challenge themselves. Was this the right decision? Was it right to put a selfish desire to provide for my family above the development of others? I didn't know, but I saw no other choice.

In the jails, my job was to keep order among inmates. L.A. County has the largest jail facilities in the United States, housing twenty-five thousand to thirty thousand inmates on a daily basis. Keeping order is essential. I broke up fights between gang members and went toe-to-toe with hardened criminals. I walked the facility with confidence as my only shield—a self-presentation born only out of self-preservation—because I did every task in the jail without my gun. Although I was assigned a firearm, custody deputies rarely wear them. It was too dangerous to carry them among the inmates, so our guns mainly stayed in our gun lockers. Instead, we were armed with handcuffs, pepper spray, and a flashlight. Fortunately, while we didn't have guns, neither did the inmates. Though many of them were dangerous, there was a certain predictability to the job—a sense of control that came from working inside a contained environment.

Patrol, however, was the exact opposite. Here, unpredictability ruled. People called us out of crisis. They were facing situations that they couldn't anticipate, contain, or handle themselves. These situations had often spiraled out of their control and required emergency help. My job on that first day was to ride along with a more experienced deputy to learn, observe, and be observed by a senior deputy.

In a patrol car, we would be dispatched via an on-board computer called a mobile digital terminal. When a call came in, the computer made a three-tone sound, and the call appeared on the computer screen with a list of codes and a small narrative giving us an idea of the situation we'd face. For more serious calls, a dispatcher would "voice" the calls over the police radio as well. I had been studying my codes, but the dispatcher spoke so fast that I was unable to comprehend what was being said. As the 902A call appeared on the computer screen of the terminal and a voice came over the police radio, I became fearfully excited. It wasn't the code I was excited about—902A meaning suicide or attempted suicide—but the chance to finally learn this aspect of my job.

"Damn." My partner grimaced and shook his head when he heard the call. "I hate calls like this," he said. But I was still so naïve, I had no clue what was coming as we headed off to deal with this crisis.

My partner put the car in park and got out. A county paramedic rescue squad, with its lights still rotating, sat silently in front of the yellow house. Several cabinet doors within the squad were already wide open. At the house, the garage door was up, and two paramedics were huddled over a person lying on the cement floor. One of the paramedics frantically applied chest compressions while the other adjusted the portable EKG machine to get the heart rate reading. My partner and I walked closer, and I craned my head to see around the paramedic's shoulder. My stomach clenched. This was a kid! A boy—maybe sixteen years old—wearing dusty jeans and a tee shirt, was lying on the floor. His thin chest moved in response to the compressions, but not because he was breathing on his own. The sight was so sobering that it took me a moment to hear it: sobbing.

I turned toward the sound. The boy's mom was standing way in the back of the garage, arms crossed in front of her body as if she was hugging herself. She was weeping uncontrollably. The physical distance that remained between her and her young son conveyed her disbelief, a refusal to accept what was occurring. No doubt, her worst fears were materializing right in front of her. Just to the left, I saw another boy, an older boy, whose shoulders shook as he watched the paramedics try to save his brother. He, too, was crying violently, shaking his head back and forth as wet, guttural noises emerged from his mouth.

My eyes drifted to the boy lying motionless on the cold cement floor. The paramedics were frantically working to reverse the child's last choice. Just behind the paramedics lay an old dirty rope. Suddenly, I realized what I was looking at: one end of the rope formed a very crudely made noose. My gaze traveled back towards the weeping mother and then to the rafters where the other half of the rope still dangled motionlessly. I could see that someone had cut the rope, one half remaining tied to the rafters and the other staying with the boy.

My partner solemnly approached the mom, but I stayed rooted in place, the scene captured in slow motion. The flat line on the EKG monitor and the grim faces of the paramedics told a story that would have a heartbreaking ending. My vision suddenly blurred as tears sprang to my eyes.

"Excuse me," I mumbled to no one in particular as I turned and quickly walked back to the patrol car. I opened the passenger door and collapsed into the seat, half in, half out of the car. He was just a boy, I thought, and now he was dead. The paramedics weren't calling it, but it was obvious he had no vital signs. They would load him onto the gurney of the arriving ambulance and take him to the hospital. His mother and brother would wait, holding out hope that some miracle would occur in the ambulance, only to find out an hour later that this young life was truly gone. I wiped the tears from my eyes and took a deep, unsteady breath. Never before had I felt so helpless in a moment that screamed for help. Never before had I felt so frustrated. Never before had I felt so inadequate. There was no way I could take another step into that garage. If there was ever a moment that needed answers, this was it—and I had none. How was a deputy sheriff—hell, how was a *human being*—supposed to handle this? I had seen death before, but never so innocent, so tragic, so unnecessary. But I had a responsibility to be there, with the family and with my partner. I took several more deep breaths to pull myself together and forced myself to walk back to the house.

There, my partner began to ask the questions that are so hard to ask but that could not be left ignored. Through her sorrow, the mother recounted what she could.

"I caught Thomas sneaking in the back door last night after midnight," she told him in a quavering voice. "He's not supposed to go out late at night," she said, with a tone that seemed to be asking if that was a valid rule. She paused for a minute, as if rewinding time, looking for answers. "I yelled at him. I told him there was no reason good enough to excuse sneaking out of the house. I grounded him. No phone, no friends, nothing. He knew the rules. He was disrespecting me by sneaking out. As punishment, I said he would spend his day cleaning the garage. Organizing it. Sweeping the floor. The whole thing."

The mother, Sarah, glanced at her older son, who continued to stare at the paramedics, who were starting an IV with epinephrine and preparing the emergency defibrillator in another attempt to jumpstart the boy's heart. "CLEAR," one said. Then *thump*. The paramedics both quickly looked at the thin ribbon of paper emerging from the EKG machine. I did not need to see the ribbon. Their reaction and frantic return to the boy told me the result.

"William came out to the garage and screamed for me," she said, nodding to her older son. "It was a horrible scream. I ran out here and saw William holding Thomas, just trying to keep him up in the air so that—" She broke down again, shaking her head, unable to speak anymore.

Eventually, the boy was transported to the local hospital. The family got into their car and followed. The garage door was shut. We finished our work and were off to the next call.

The boy, Thomas, didn't make it. The mom and the rest of the family were left with only questions. Why did Thomas kill himself? What was so bad, so horrible, that he didn't see any other option but to take his own life?

The boy's mother may never have found out, but I did. It was information that made the situation all the more tragic.

In addition to my job as a deputy sheriff, I also worked with a youth group. Some of the kids in the youth group knew Thomas. Together, they had put together bits and pieces of his story and told me what had happened as they understood it. Thomas and his girlfriend had recently broken up. He was shaken up over it and trying to repair the relationship. In a desperate move, he snuck out of his house late at night and went to her house. She didn't want him there, the kids from the youth group told me. She harshly stated that she was in no way interested in getting back together. Then, for some unknown reason, she lied, telling him she was pregnant. He was going to be in trouble for that. He returned home in an emotional crisis, only to be caught sneaking back in to the house by his mother. She blew up because he'd broken a rule and snuck out late. How, then, would he ever be able to discuss the much bigger, more important issues of his life?

As we pulled away from the yellow house, I swore to myself that I would do whatever I could to prevent such a thing from happening again. I had no answers then, but I committed myself to finding something, anything, that could spare another family from such an event. There *had* to be solutions that could prevent these moments filled with regret.

My thoughts turned to my own children. Although my oldest was just six, I wondered what that boy, Thomas, had been like when he was that age. As for my children, was I asking the right questions of them? Had I created an environment where they could talk to me about anything, anytime? What did I need to change in my own life to prevent the same tragedy from occurring in my home? I wanted more than just answers. I wanted workable solutions that I could share with other parents before crisis consumed them.

More than fifteen years later, I remember Thomas. I remember his family and his story, as well as my tearful reaction to it. It resonates with me as I see similar stories play out time and time again. Fortunately, they do not all end in suicide, but many of them result in deep emotional damage. And many of the people who inflict that emotional damage are the very people charged with loving and protecting them: the parents. I believe Sarah had no intention of pushing her child to this end. She clearly loved Thomas. But she was understandably furious with him for sneaking out. She was furious at him for making her worry, even for an instant, about his safety.

She was furious at him for making her realize that she couldn't control or protect him. She was furious because she didn't even know he had been gone. That fury, that combination of frustration and sadness, made Sarah want to punish Thomas. Not just discipline him as a result of him breaking the rules, but *punish* him because he had cost Sarah her own peace of mind. In the moments when Thomas returned home, consumed with his own crisis, his mother's anger, frustration, and rejection may have been all he heard.

Sarah isn't so different from the rest of us. The emotional cocktail we feel when a child misbehaves is just the tip of the iceberg. Many of these emotions take on the look and sound of anger. Underneath that anger is frustration. Underneath that frustration is fear. It is fear for the child's safety or future . . . and fear of failing as parents.

Think about it. When a toddler collapses on the floor of a grocery store in the middle of a temper tantrum, many parents are mortified at the idea of their child behaving like such a . . . a . . . a child! But these are the moments that define us as parents. Do we respond angrily, demanding instant compliance from a child who is so overwrought and overwhelmed that he can't control his emotions or behavior? Do we blush and look around to see if other people are looking at us critically? Do we allow our child to manipulate our behavior? Or is there another response we can give that communicates something else? What if—instead of scooping up the child with an angry sigh and rushing from the store—we sit down on the floor right next to our son or daughter, presenting a calm presence and giving that child time and space to handle his or her emotions? But we are often stopped by the unarticulated fear that other parents will come up and say, "What's wrong with your child?" or "Can't you control your son?" or "When my children were young, they would have *never* behaved like that!" What is really controlling our behavior as a parent? Is it our child's tantrum, or our fear of rejection from other adults? Should we let our fears enable our children's dysfunctional behavior?

Fast forward to a parent/teacher conference for a middle school child.

"Amy isn't turning in her homework," the teacher says. "I've talked with her about it several times, and she always promises to bring it in, but when I ask her about it, she says she left it at home."

"I can't believe she's not turning it in," we might say. "She is in her room all evening doing her homework, or so she says. She must be on the computer or on her phone. I've told her over and over again to get her homework done first. Don't worry. I'll make sure her homework is turned in from now on!"

No doubt, although we are concerned about Amy not doing well in school, there is also the feeling of embarrassment, the fear that the teacher believes we are not keeping order at home. This is the feeling that is most likely to guide the conversation with Amy that evening versus trying to problem-solve to get to the root of why Amy isn't getting her homework done.

Picture getting a call from the local police station, telling you to come and pick up your thirteen-year-old son, who was caught shoplifting. On the ride to the police station, questions naturally crowd your mind. How long has this been going on? What friends are influencing your son? How did you not know? What kind of long-term effect will this have on the boy? What will the neighbors, family, and school think when they find out? That fear of being ashamed by a child's actions will very likely supersede any other emotion when you finally get in a room with the child, and the conversation will not be pleasant.

The very real danger—as Sarah found out—is that when we, as parents, ride that tide of fear, we feel vindicated by the need to punish our children in their time of crisis instead of working to understand and help them. We tend to talk *at* our children instead of *with* them. It's usually not intentional, but that doesn't make a difference. The effect is the same: we damage our children. We make them think they don't matter. We tell them, by our actions, that we're more concerned with how others perceive us than about our children's well-being. Each time we do that, we chip away at their self-worth and their implicit sense of trust in us to protect them, to care for them, and to be their champion.

Sometimes, if recognized, this emotional damage can be repaired. But sometimes we don't get a second chance. Sarah didn't get one with Thomas. That's why we can't wait until a major crisis occurs to show our children they matter. It's something that must be done every day.

We tend to TALK at our children instead of with THEM.

Don't get me wrong; this is not always easy. As our kids' problems become bigger, whether it's because they use drugs, become a gang member, get pregnant, or drop out of school, the typical parental instinct is to fear. But acting on that fear in a way that tears down our kids doesn't help them or their relationship with us. On the other hand, being able to approach them from a position of love—not fear—provides us with the understanding and perspective we need to truly make a difference.

BROKERS OF HOPE

DISILLUSIONED TO THE CORE

· CHAPTER 6 ·

AFTER TWO AND A HALF YEARS ON PATROL, I HAD SEEN A LOT. I'd experienced the thrill and fear of chasing bad guys down dark alleys, of arresting drug dealers, burglars, and murderers. But the cases that got to me the most were the ones involving kids. Parents called us because they could no longer control their situation and wanted us to change their kids. I saw runaways, as well as kids involved in vandalism, burglaries, robberies, suicides, and homicides. It didn't take long for me to discover I couldn't help them. I could talk to them, I could detain or arrest them, but I couldn't actually change their behavior. And the kids knew it. They realized early on that they could manipulate the juvenile justice system and that it gave them second and third chances. They saw that "no" didn't really mean no, so what incentive did they have to change? They were disrespectful, and I was ineffective. This wasn't what I thought I would be doing or should be doing. This wasn't the way I thought I would make a difference.

"Rent-A-Dad" calls were among the most frustrating. These were calls from people, usually single moms, who had reached their often-considerable limit in dealing with their kids and called the police for help. One mom called us because her daughter had taken twenty dollars from the mom's purse. The mom and daughter had a heated argument and the mom called the police, asking us to make the daughter give her back her twenty dollars. My partner and I showed up at their house. It seemed like a "normal" middle-class single-parent home. We talked with them for ten to fifteen minutes, trying to calm them both down. Mom didn't want her daughter arrested for the theft, and the daughter just wanted mom's attention. When they at last begrudgingly agreed to try to work it out, with the daughter returning the twenty dollars, we left, knowing that we had only put a bandage on a situation that required surgery. How bad is it that you'll call the police for help managing your child? And how much can we actually solve during a call?

That family needed much more time and work than we were allotted, trained for, or prepared to give them. I was seeing the worst of the "quick-fix" society as it took its toll on children through quick-fix parenting.

Along with this increasing feeling of impotence, the tragedy and violence that we dealt with left a residue of hopelessness in me.

One particular call we handled tormented me for a long time. A man left his house early one morning while his wife and three children were still sleeping. He was meeting some friends to go hunting. Somehow, he had gotten distracted and ran a red light. He hit another car and died instantly.

The sun was just coming up when I knocked on the family's door. The street was quiet, and the sound of my knuckles on the door echoed in the street. A relative had called the wife and told her that he thought he saw a truck just like her husband's involved in a bad wreck. She called the hospital but they referred her to our desk. Our desk wouldn't say anything over the phone, and when the news was confirmed, my fellow officer, Janie, and I were sent out to deliver it. I believe the wife already had a pretty good idea that she was caught up in the middle of her worst nightmare.

I heard someone moving on the other side of the door and realized the wife was looking out the peephole. That was when she started screaming. She had a diagnosed panic disorder that she would disclose to us soon enough—but for now, all she could do was yell "NO, NO, NO!"

"Mrs. Williamson? Cynthia Williamson?" I asked in a controlled voice.

She nodded, opening the door slowly. She leaned on the door for support and pressed a trembling hand against her mouth. She had put all the pieces together, but our presence only affirmed what she did not want to accept. We helped her over to a chair at the dining room table and stood there as she wept. She wanted to know everything, but neither one of us was going to give her all the details; it wouldn't help her grief, and my heart just could not bear it. This was horrendous enough.

"Is there anyone who can come here and stay with you?" Janie asked, even as the woman continued to wail. As her cries filled the painfully normal space of her family's dining room, I suddenly, heavily, understood the biblical phrase *lamentations of the women.*

After several long minutes, her wails turned into quieter sobs. "What am I supposed to do? I don't know what to do!"

"Who can come and be with you, Mrs. Williamson? Do you have a family member or a friend? A neighbor?" Janie probed.

"I have family and friends from my church," she said finally, her hands shaking in her lap.

"Can you call and ask them to come over?" Janie asked.

Childlike, she nodded. "Okay, I'll call." She excused herself to the front room to make the call. From there, we could hear her cry again as reality set in. A few minutes later, she returned, eyes red, with tissues in her hand.

"My friend will come over, but it will take her awhile. She lives on the other side of town," she said. Then we heard voices coming from upstairs. Cynthia looked up at me in fresh horror, tears flooding her eyes once more. "The kids," she said. "I don't know how to tell them about their daddy. Please."

She looked at me urgently as footsteps traipsed down the stairs. "Please, you tell them."

"Ma'am, I think that would be better coming from you," I tried to explain. I looked around the room at the mantle displaying a vignette of family photos. They had been a happy family of five, with the dad, the mom, and the three kids. My heart panged with the realization that those three kids, those kids who had just lost their dad, were about the same age as my own three children: seven, four, and one. Those kids were about to hear the worst news they may ever hear in their lives, and their mom wanted me to deliver it.

"Please," she pleaded as the kids came bouncing downstairs. Two girls and a boy, blonde like their mom, stopped and sat down on the bottom stair. They fell quiet when they saw their teary-eyed mom and me. Their eyes took in my uniform, the gun on one hip, and the radio on the other, making its usual noises. The little boy took a quick step behind the oldest girl, shyly peeking out.

I didn't want to do this, but how could I say no? The wife had so many hard days in front of her, and then difficult years as a single parent after that. I looked at my partner, who shrugged. I sighed. And as I somberly walked over to the three kids and sat next to them on the staircase, a chill speared through me. I felt as if I were telling my own children about my death. I took a deep breath, looked into their beautiful, curious eyes, and broke the news that would effectively end their childhood.

That night, and many nights after, I couldn't sleep. Every time I closed my eyes, I heard that poor woman's mournful, unrelenting sorrow. The only way I could get to sleep was by drinking a bottle of wine. It wasn't the ideal way to cope, but it was the only way I could. I told Mel about this situation, and she understood that I was struggling. My now familiar feeling of helplessness was coupled this time with the realization of my own mortality. As a deputy sheriff, I was responsible for protecting people—for helping people—and it ate away at me when I was repeatedly in situations where I was not able to do either. That frustration grew, yet I seldom shared how I felt with anyone. It was actually unusual that I shared my pain from that horrible call with my wife. Some of the calls I had been on, the heartbreak I'd seen, I just didn't want to bring into my home. I didn't want Mel or the kids to even imagine what I had seen.

My situation was not unusual, and that dichotomy may be why there is such a high degree of divorce, alcoholism, and suicide among people in law enforcement. We are attracted to the job because we want to make things better, but too often, we simply can't. For me, it was nearly impossible to empathize with others' pain without completely taking it on. It was equally impossible to separate myself from others' pain without becoming completely callous. I could be the tough guy, but I wasn't designed to be. I was designed to care. But to care without being able to truly make things better was grinding me down. I needed a change. I could not keep using a bottle to cope, so I signed up for counseling sessions to learn some new coping skills. Eventually, I was able to make peace with the lady screaming in my dreams. But the reality of not being able to make a real difference remained the same.

THE only thing I ever witnessed that created LONG-TERM change was SPEAKING LOUDLY into these young lives about Love, acceptance, AND Hope.

My chance to make a change came by surprise, when my captain decided to accompany me on a ride-along. He didn't tell me why, and I didn't ask. He simply took off the metal insignias on his collar to be a less noticeable target for violence and sat in the front seat of my patrol car one evening. It was awkward. What was my captain doing in my patrol car? What the hell was I supposed to do? He didn't say, and I knew better than to ask.

It was December 1999, and the L.A. County Sheriff's Department was undergoing a philosophical change. We were tired of repeatedly arresting juveniles. We were realizing that arresting kids didn't change their behavior. In east L.A., two deputies, Vincent Romero and Drew Birtness, had jumped out in the lead of this new mindset. They, too, were frustrated, realizing they were arresting the kids and grandkids of juveniles the deputies had arrested in years past. They wanted to stop the vicious cycle. Romero and Birtness began a program in 1996 called VIDA, or Vital Intervention and Directional Alternatives Program, a multi-week program to help at-risk kids change their behavior by making better choices. They were looking to stop the generational dysfunction that seemed to be compounding across the county. My captain had been instructed to start a VIDA program for our area of Los Angeles. When a new position within the program had opened up, a note had gone out to the department to see who was interested. I had said I was interested, and although I didn't know it at the time, the night my captain accompanied me on patrol was my job interview. When he offered me the job, I grabbed the opportunity.

There was no doubt that this would be a challenge. Even though no funds were available to start the program, the captain wanted me to get it going in thirty days. So, with eight photocopied sheets of paper with basic instructions on how to start a VIDA site, my new partner, Johnny Jones, and I began.

The first few days, Johnny and I just drove around neighborhoods, searching for a rent-free location since we didn't have a budget. Once we found a building, we'd still need to flesh out the structure of the program, find people to help run it, and let community agencies know about it so they could recommend participants. While that certainly made our task difficult, it also forced us to be creative and innovative. As a result, we often collaborated with strange bedfellows. For example, we had parolees and ex-cons who lined up to help. These hardcore men and women who had made their mistakes and been through the system passionately wanted to keep kids out of jail. They talked with young people about personal value and not letting past slips define their future course. They brought their "street cred" to our classroom to tell kids why they should listen to those who cared about them. It was enlightening and hopeful to see that no matter what side of crime you were on, there was a united message to help. Still, with every successful step forward, it could take four months to get a refill printer ink cartridge our VIDA deputies needed.

When I first started with VIDA, I was looking forward to a change from patrol, a chance to make a positive impact, but what may have influenced me even more was the notion that I was *chosen* for this position. I was special. I mattered. As time went on and the program began to take on shape and life, parents started thanking me for giving them their family back, for *saving* them. Parents of students in our graduating VIDA class made up little awards for us, and the families signed them. I realized with some surprise that for the first time in my career, I was actually making a difference.

In the next three years, I helped develop the Antelope Valley VIDA site into an effective sixteen-week program that accepted kids aged eleven through seventeen, helping them make the transition from childhood to adulthood with lessons on everything from hygiene to career planning, academic achievement, dealing with substance use, and effectively communicating with parents. In the early years, we were still learning the many aspects of juvenile intervention. The "Scared Straight" dogma was still around, and while many thought that kids just needed a taste of fear in order to behave, the only thing I ever witnessed that created long-term change was speaking loudly into these young lives about love, acceptance, and hope. At least four hundred families came through our site during that time, and as much as they experienced change, I changed, too. I went from selfishly seeking validation to realizing that *I* was the one who needed to validate these young lives. We saw so much dysfunction, so much victimization, so much tragedy, and what we learned from it all was that these kids just wanted to matter. They would do just about anything to feel important.

We worked with fourteen-year-old girls who were prostituting to pay for meth to shoot in their veins, with young men trying to bully their mothers around the home, and with twelfth graders failing because they couldn't read. The more we breathed belief into them, the more they disclosed to us. The more they disclosed, the more our hearts broke. While we worked with the children, we also worked with the parents. We heard the stories of how these families ended up in crisis. We were becoming brokers of hope.

Over time, I began incorporating lessons from work into my own parenting style. I saw the importance of creating an environment where conversations could and would occur. Both in VIDA and in my own home, we were making a measurable difference. And then, in January 2003, the program abruptly ended when the federal government cancelled the grants that funded the personnel. Just as quickly as it was created, VIDA was dissolved across the board. The fourteen sites closed, and the thirty deputies who worked with VIDA were reassigned back to patrol. What was in the best interest of the kids was not as important as politics or budget. I was bitterly disappointed. We were just starting to build momentum for change, and now, with a stroke of some politician's pen on a budgetary line item, it was over.

I went back on patrol and found that my patience and tolerance for bullshit, violence, and tragedy was greatly diminished. One night, I ended up in a high-speed pursuit of a suspect who was trying to load a firearm even as he fled from us. The call initiated as no big deal: a suspicious person was walking around a neighborhood. As we pulled into the development of tract houses, my partner ran the license plates of cars parked along the street. Soon enough, one came back from an address in Kern County, which was thirty miles north. All the other cars were registered to homes in the neighborhood. This outlier raised suspicion. So we parked down the block with our lights off and just waited. Sure enough, out came our burglar with his arms full of loot. We pulled up on him and tried to detain him, but he immediately ran. We surrounded large areas of the neighborhood, but he still escaped. Six hours later, he had stolen another car. He was headed to Kern County with us right behind him. Flying at dangerous speeds, we put our lives on the line to catch him, but cuffing him brought me no satisfaction: by tomorrow, there would be another one. This pattern was never going to end.

Not many weeks later, I sat in my black and white, contemplating the apartment I could see from my car window. My chest felt swollen and tight as I wondered how something like this latest tragedy could have happened. The station had received a tip that an eighteen-month-old baby may have been killed. The tip contained only limited information with vague descriptions of the possible location, so in between other calls for service that night, another deputy and I tried to match up the description to a location based on our knowledge of the area.

Around two o'clock in the morning, we finally found the apartment building matching the caller's tip. There, we saw a woman carrying a laundry basket of what looked like baby clothes. She was walking straight toward the apartment number we were looking for. We emerged from our separate cars and approached her, starting a conversation. As our investigation progressed and we entered the apartment, we realized that there was, in fact, a baby missing from the residence; you could still smell the cleaning solution wafting from the baby's empty crib. As the night wore on, another unit apprehended the father . . . with the baby's burned and tortured body stuffed in a duffel bag hidden in the rear of his vehicle. We discovered that the couple had murdered their eighteen-month old baby, and we were standing in the room where it had happened only hours ago. All of us working on the investigation felt sick in our hearts and stomachs at the horrific nature of this crime. Even after my shift ended, I sat in the car outside the apartment complex, contemplating the evil we had seen. Questions screamed in my head: what can I do to prevent other parents from abusing their children? How do we intervene in young, abused lives? What can I do to save the next child before it's too late?

Ironically, or maybe through divine intervention, my phone rang as I sat in my car. The sky was beginning to lighten when I answered the call from Operations Bureau, Office of Homeland Security.

"I've got a job for you," Captain Johnson announced. "I believe you have the skill set needed to bring VIDA back."

I was shocked. Only three months had passed since the program had been disbanded, and I assumed it was over forever, but apparently, the political wind had shifted. Captain Johnson named some incentives, such as a laptop and an unmarked car, not knowing how little those things mattered to me right then. "I need to know if you're in," he said.

Although my previous experience with VIDA and my work as a sheriff's deputy, a wilderness guide, and a Marine helped me qualify for this position, I understood that if I declined, Captain Johnson would just go to the next person on some list he had sitting in front of him. How long would this position last? I wanted to talk it over with Mel, but Captain Johnson repeated that he needed to know right then. Could I risk VIDA ending again, tossing me back to patrol? Could I risk *not* being involved with VIDA again, this time improving the program and using it to truly target the kids who needed it most? I looked back at the apartment, watching as deputies began stringing the yellow crime tape up around the front door.

"Yes," I said to Captain Johnson. "Yes, I'll take the job."

THERE IS A DANGEROUS **gap** BeTWEEN PARENT ⟨and⟩ *CHILD.* a **gap** SPREAD by **FEAR** instead of **CLOSED** by **LOVE.**

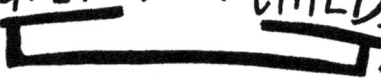

DESPERATE
FOR A
LIFELINE

THE FIRST VIDA PROGRAM HAD BEEN CREATED BY OUR HEARTS, GROWN FROM THE SEEDS OF EIGHT PIECES OF PAPER. And although we did good work, my captain instructed me that this version of the program needed to be better. Smarter. I now knew that VIDA could be sacrificed at a whim by a politician's budget, but until then, I had a feeling of renewal, of possibility.

In Los Angeles, the sheriff's department and the police in general have long had a good reputation with the public. However, there are those moments when the public's trust is challenged. Some of it is natural—nobody likes getting in trouble when they've done something wrong—but some of that mistrust we earned through our own failings. We tended to react to juvenile delinquency the same way we reacted to criminal behavior: we were opposing forces standing on different sides of some moral compass. We "attacked" the delinquency problem with a mindset that these kids just wanted to be criminals. This, of course, was false. As we set out to redevelop the program, I knew that several things needed to change. First and foremost was our own mindset about kids in trouble. Children did not want to fail, and when they did, we needed to do better than blame them for the results.

As the list of groups and institutions that needed to change their mindsets grew, I saw I had my work cut out for me. VIDA was going to become a vehicle to create change not only in kids, but also in parents, teachers, probation officers, law enforcement, and anyone who worked with troubled youth. But first, we had to rebuild the program on founded, evidence-based principles and academic research. Cognitive psychology, the study and knowledge of how and what we think, would become a keystone to changing mindsets. The more I learned about the science, the more I understood: all of my values and beliefs are based in cognitive psychology.

In so many of my experiences, whether as a child, a wilderness instructor, a Marine, or a deputy, I could see the psychological roots that made people react the way they did. For example, as an adult, I can look back and understand that some of my parents' behaviors were rooted in their own insecurity and fear. As a wilderness instructor, I often helped people push past their self-imposed limiting beliefs by challenging them physically to overcome their fears. As a Marine, I learned the importance of working cohesively. Now, as a deputy, I could see the deep hurt and disconnect that was destroying families. There was, and still is, a dangerous gap growing between parent and child—a gap spread by fear instead of closed by love.

"My kid won't listen," parents complained to me, frustrated and angry.

"My parents don't listen," kids said to me, trying to act cool but feeling raw.

The VIDA program was designed to help kids learn anger management and social, communication, and coping skills. Even in the program's early days, parents would barrel through our doors, hauling Junior to stand in front of me. The kid wasn't going to school, or was failing school, or had just been caught shoplifting or some other non-violent misdemeanor.

"Fix him," the parents begged.

They were in crisis and had a hard time seeing anything objectively. Instead of recognizing that what they were doing with the kid wasn't working, they assumed the problem was the child. The child wasn't getting it, and the refusal to understand had to be intentional. The solution? Fix the kid. They didn't consider that maybe the way they were communicating or *what* they were communicating was the problem. No, the kid just doesn't listen. And parents seemed stuck in this belief. Even parents who wanted to do right by their kids, who cared about them and wanted the best for them, fell into this trap.

But I'll say it again: children don't dream of failing. It's not part of their makeup.

The explanation for this dichotomy between wanting to succeed and still failing came to me as a life lesson presented on a napkin. Soon after we initiated VIDA 2.0, I was at lunch with a colleague and good friend, Richard Weintraub. Richard was assisting me on the VIDA redevelopment project. We'd had several conversations regarding how to teach some of the academic theories so parents could implement them in their lives. During lunch, we talked about how to teach human emotions so people could get some useful insight from the lesson. Richard grabbed a pen from his pocket and pulled one of the napkins from the table in front of him. Then he looked up at me.

"If we boiled *all* human emotion down in a big pot, we would end up with the two primary ones," he said. "What are they, Mark?"

"Anger?" I guessed inaccurately.

Richard coaxed me closer and closer until we had it down. LOVE and FEAR. Those were the two primary human emotions. That was when Richard started to draw on the napkin. He drew two trees; on one trunk, he wrote LOVE, and on the other, he wrote FEAR. He once again looked up at me and smiled. "Now, I want you to tell me *all* of the corresponding emotions that we would find on the Tree of Fear."

As I called them out, he wrote them down: "Hate, anger, rejection, insecurity, anxiety, loneliness, apathy . . ." The list went on. Then we did the same for the LOVE tree. "Acceptance," I began. "Security, peace, joy, empathy . . ."

Richard continued. "Mark, if we respond to a fear emotion with another fear emotion, we just continue the cycle of fear, but if we can learn to respond to a fear emotion with a love emotion, we can begin to break a very poisonous emotional cycle."

That was one of the most important lessons I've ever learned.

As I looked at the rough sketch of the trees, I remembered Thomas, the boy who committed suicide in his garage, and his mother, Sarah. Her worry that her son had snuck out late at night—and her fear that she could not control him—showed up on the branches of the tree as anger. That anger pushed a boy who was feeling emotionally fragile to his breaking point. We all know the Tree of Fear, and we all want to know the Tree of Love. How do we tell our children no in such a way that we communicate that they matter without them hearing that *we do not care*?

I couldn't help but ask myself: how many times had parents struck out in fear in ways that, to the child, sounded and felt like anger and rejection? My own parents were a textbook example. With the hindsight of distance and maturity, I wondered whether the way they behaved toward me was due to of a lack of knowledge about parenting, exacerbated by a fear that they or I would fail. When my father told me I would never amount to anything, could it be that he doubted whether he had the wisdom to help me become something? When my mother threw things at me, beat me, or screamed at me, could that have come from her own treatment as a child and her own frustrations with being a parent? I didn't know, but even the possibility that their behavior toward me could be caused by something *unrelated to me* rocked me back on my heels.

Over the rest of that lunch, Richard continued to talk about love. "It starts with a desire to understand, not condemn. Think about it—when most parents find that their child has gotten in trouble, what's the first reaction?"

"Anger," I said immediately.

"That's right, often based on the inconvenience the child has caused; now you have to pay for the window that was broken or you have to leave work early to pick Junior up from school. And sometimes the anger is followed by embarrassment. How could your child have done this to you? Fear, of course, is a huge knee-jerk response," Richard continued. "Fear that the child is out of control. Fear that he's associated with the wrong people or going down the wrong path. Fear that this kid will make you look like a bad parent."

CHILDREN DO NOT WANT to FAIL. BUT WHEN THEY DO, we need to do BETTER THAN BLAME THEM for the Results.

I nodded. I had seen these reactions played out many times, both on patrol and in VIDA. I had even seen it played out between my own children and me.

"But when you approach a situation from the Tree of Love, your perspective isn't about how this is affecting you, but *why* the child is behaving like this. Your approach is rooted in finding out why. What is in the child's belief structure that guides him to this behavior? And through understanding, honesty, and support, how can we help change his behavior?"

Over the years, I have referred to that napkin drawing over and over. Many times, a kid who was confounding his parents or teachers with his behavior came into our program. His parents thought they had tried everything. Crying. Yelling. Incentives. Punishments. Threats. But the behavior continued.

One mother came to us pleading. Her teenage daughter was a habitual runaway. The mom had tried everything, but periodically, the girl would just disappear for a week. The mother was beside herself, and we understood. We knew only too well the dangers awaiting a young girl on the street. But when the police found the girl and picked her up, their only recourse was to take her home. There was nothing else they had jurisdiction to do. This situation repeated itself until finally a deputy sat down, talked with the girl, and really *listened*, not from the Tree of Fear but from the Tree of Love. Turns out, the girl was avoiding her lecherous stepfather, whose job kept him away for a week at a time. When he came home, the girl ran away. Once we started asking the right questions, ones that weren't based in fear, the girl was able to confide in us and we were able to rectify the situation. But it also changed the narrative. The girl wasn't a "habitual runaway." She was trying to protect herself as best she could. But we could only see that from the vantage point of the Tree of Love.

This young girl's story isn't unique. Remember David, the kid who didn't see any point in going to school because he figured he'd be dead or in jail in a few years anyway? His mother came to us, understandably, from the Tree of Fear. What kind of future did David have if he ran with gangs? How could she ensure his safety when he wouldn't listen to her? How could she control his life when he didn't care what she said? It wasn't until we stopped talking to David from the Tree of Fear and asked questions from the Tree of Love that we began to understand David's perspective. At that point, we could start helping him figure out steps to a different future.

The Tree of Fear and the Tree of Love laid the groundwork for how we approach kids in VIDA. But to truly give parents the tools to understand how children think, what they need, and how the parents could change their own behaviors and those of their children, I still had more work to do.

PEOPLE — adults + — children ↑
will LIVE UP ↑
OR DOWN
to our
EXPECTATIONS. ↓

NO LICENSE REQUIRED

WHEN MY DAUGHTER MEGAN WAS BORN, I REMEMBER LOOKING DOWN AT HER WITHIN THE SNUGLY WRAPPED HOSPITAL RECEIVING BLANKET. Her scrunched up face indicated her indignity at being forced into this world of bright lights and noise. She was light in my arms as I rocked her back and forth, taking in every detail of her little face. "I'm your daddy," I whispered.

I glanced behind me to check on Mel, who dozed in the hospital bed. For the moment, it was just my daughter and me. Obviously, I wasn't the first person in the world to become a parent, but it felt like it. I've always believed in God and His miracles, but this gift that I so carefully held was more amazing than I could have ever imagined.

"I will always love you," I promised Megan as I kissed her wrinkled forehead. Her mouth stretched wide in a yawn as she gazed back at me, unimpressed. I chuckled. She was wise beyond her hours.

When Megan was born, I was still in the yearlong background checking process before being hired as a deputy. I didn't know this at the time, but it would be two more weeks before I'd get the invitation to come aboard. I was still conducting wilderness hikes and filling in hours at the local In-N-Out Burger. Mel and I had been happy improvising our lives, but as soon as we found out we had a baby on the way, we craved stability. When the sheriff's job approval came, I was happy to take it.

"Hey, Megan," I said to her softly, as if she would respond. She was starting to fall asleep. Already, I'd noticed my voice getting higher and higher as I talked to her. I was cooing to her. It was not intentional. I couldn't quite seem to say anything without taking on that silly singsong voice, but I had so much to say to her, to share with her.

Had my parents ever cuddled and cooed over me? Somehow, I doubted it. I always felt like an inconvenience to them rather than a miracle. Megan would never feel as if she didn't matter, I vowed. I would make sure of that.

My promise was sincere, and throughout my career as a sheriff on patrol and with VIDA, I encountered many parents who probably said the same thing. They looked at their own tiny, defenseless little bundles and promised that they would always love and protect them. But why doesn't that always happen? Good parenting is certainly one of the world's hardest jobs, and it is ironic that it's a job that just about anyone can get without filling out an application or having an interview, without a background investigation, a typing test, training, or a check for references. Even when parents have the best intentions, so many opportunities exist to do it wrong.

I'm not immune.

A few years later, as I opened my front door, my kids ran to me with open arms. "Daddy!" they yelled. It had been a sixteen-hour day in a string of long days. I looked forward to Megan, now nine, Matthew, aged six, and Madison, the baby at three, but I was exhausted after my shift. I didn't want to talk about my day, I didn't want to ask about theirs, and I didn't want to sit down at the dinner table. All I craved at that moment was silence and solitude.

"Daddy, come see what we did in art!" Megan said, grabbing my hand to hustle me inside the door.

The headache that I had kept at bay all day bloomed, pounding in my temples.

"Daddy, can we play a game, please?" Matthew begged. I knew he especially looked forward to having another male in the house, and although I tried to spend time with all of the kids, I made sure to spend some extra "guy time" with him.

Madison threw her arms around my leg and curled up, making it hard to walk.

"Look, guys, I just got home," I snapped. "Could I just get a minute before everybody wants something from me?" I dropped Megan's hand and moved Madison's arms from my leg. I took two steps toward the sanctuary of my bedroom, when I stopped, realizing how quiet it was. In the silence, I replayed my own words.

"Sorry, Daddy," Megan said, her voice barely audible.

I turned to look at my precious children, the ones I had promised that I would always love and would always let know they mattered. In less than a minute, I had destroyed their enthusiasm—about seeing me! In just a few inconsiderate words, I had effectively conveyed that I was not as excited to see them after a long day as they were to see me. That they weren't important to me. That they didn't matter. That wasn't what I had meant to do, but that was what I got across all the same.

I hung my head, and then crouched down next to them. "Kids," I said, opening my arms. And, bless them, just like that, they scooted in close. I wrapped my arms around all three of them.

"I'm sorry. I shouldn't have acted like that," I said. "I'm really tired, and that made me grumpy. But you're important, and I want to hear about your day, too."

To be ready to hear about my kids' day, to be ready to be Daddy, I still needed a little time after getting home. "How about when I get home, I go into my room for a while and you guys keep playing, and after a few minutes, I'll come out and we can spend the evening together?" I suggested.

They nodded, happy with that arrangement. They didn't care so much that they saw me the first minute I got home. They just wanted my attention and to know I cared. Even at their young age, they understood that I was interested in them, but I needed the personal space first in order to be fully present later. Being upfront with them helped set the foundation for that new system, and they understood that they mattered.

As my kids grew up, the parenting lessons we taught at VIDA often intersected with the homegrown lessons we developed in our house. (They have since been dubbed Cripe-isms.) At VIDA, we taught parents to communicate clearly with their kids, to talk *with* their children and not *at* their children. I taught concepts like confronting behaviors but affirming the child. I taught them not just what to do and what not to do, but *why*. We sometimes think that advising our children on the best course of action is enough, but kids have curious minds and can't help but wonder why. Nurturing that and helping them think for themselves takes longer, but ultimately, it helps them mature.

getting to know YOUR CHILD is one of the most ESSENTIAL STEPS we can take to create LASTING CHANGE

When our kids were young, Mel and I disagreed about the best way to keep them from getting too close to the wood-burning stove. Mel constantly told the kids, "No! Don't touch the stove." I preferred a different approach.

"The stove is hot," I explained. I would let them put their hand close enough to feel the heat and understand that I was trying to protect them. Despite our warnings, I knew at some point, one of the kids would touch the stove and get burned. Even though I couldn't protect them from getting hurt, I helped them understand what would happen, and afterwards, why it did happen, which is different from just telling them no.

When Mel and I became parents, I was determined that we wouldn't be the kind of parents that mine were. We said there was no way that we would beat our kids, the way my mom did until she was out of breath. I told my kids that the worst they would ever get from me was three swats on the butt. Rarely did I even need to do that because I saw that it wasn't the swat that made the kids behave. They hated to hear the disappointment in my voice when I thought they could have made better decisions. They instinctively sought to please me, so although we've had hiccups here and there, for the most part, the kids feel they can come to us when they need to.

Most of the kids in VIDA have far more challenges than my own kids do. Many come from single-parent households, where lack of education, income, and role models are the norm. Gangs, drugs, and violence are often obstacles VIDA kids have to overcome on an everyday basis. This is all the more reason to implement some essential skills and tools to strengthen the parent/child relationship and create an arena for open communication. One of the most effective techniques I've found is a family government.

In our house, I told the kids I had two main rules: I didn't want anyone to get hurt, and I didn't want anything broken. With that as a foundation, it was easier to maintain perspective when something went wrong. For all other decisions, we established a family government. I had the kids create rules and determine what the consequences would be for breaking them. With them in charge, they knew that even though we might discipline them, it would be fair. They knew the consequence wasn't because I was mad at them and wanted to wallop them to vent my anger. Discipline is not about fighting. It's actually a positive interchange designed to inspire better choices.

My son, Matthew, once broke one of the house rules, and after we talked about it, I asked, "What's the consequence for that?"

"It's a thirty-minute timeout," he said, according to the rules of the family government. "But can you just give me a swat, get it over with?" My son's ability to process what he did, understand that there was a deserving consequence, and accept it without question showed me there was no need for either a swat or a timeout. After all, the rules are about learning and being aware of boundaries. He showed me that he got it. Our conversation was very calm as he accepted full responsibility for his choices.

Family government is something that can work in all families, and I teach its creation to parents, as well as to teachers and principals, who want to reduce friction by increasing empowerment. The concept is simple: everyone gets a voice. Families talk about topics of concern, and everyone is allowed to voice opinions without fear of retaliation. The family agrees upon rules, boundaries, and fair consequences. These meetings become a pressure valve for stresses that would otherwise go unaddressed and could result in harmful behaviors or choices.

In a family government, the group holds each member accountable for behaviors. Sometimes, as parents, we are blind to ways we communicate negative messages to our children. During one of our family government meetings, Mel was upset at the kids for not cleaning up the kitchen. The kids responded that she left a big coffee mess each morning, which made them think that a clean kitchen was not terribly important after all. Mel was not aware of the example she was demonstrating. We then discussed solutions, not who was at fault. What can Mom do to stop the coffee mess and model her desire for a clean kitchen? The kids were also keen to point out some of my habits as well, like when I threw my jacket on the couch or emptied my pockets on the kitchen counter—creating the clutter I admonished them for making—and they were right. Just like Mel, I was unintentionally sending a double message. If we want our children to respond positively to feedback, so must we. I had to model my willingness to correct the behavior.

This same concept worked in a seven-day course I created for a local school district. The class, which was for the entire faculty, was based on concepts taken from our forty-hour Juvenile Intervention Instructors Course, coupled with a cognitive psychology course called 21 Keys, designed for parents and teachers by The Pacific Institute.

A particular continuation middle school in this school district was beyond troubled. Deputies didn't even want to respond there unless six more deputies were going, too. The school had between fifty and one hundred kids who were so disruptive they couldn't even eat together at lunchtime because they would end up in a huge brawl. The teachers and administrators were overwhelmed and frustrated, and the parents were angry because they wanted their kids to have a decent education in a safe place. During the seven-day course, we spoke about the concepts behind family government, and then the principal applied those concepts when he met with the parents.

"What do you think should be the most important rules at this school?" he asked the crowded meeting room.

"No fighting," one parent said.

The principal wrote it down.

"No drugs. No weapons," someone else suggested.

"No bullying," said another person.

The principal wrote down all of the rules the parents called out. It was a long list. The principal then handed the parents green sticky dots to put by the rules they deemed most important. The items with the most dots became the school rules, and the parents immediately became invested in supporting them. (In reality, the parents came up with the same rules that are common on most school campuses, but they now had ownership of the boundaries, so supporting them was easy.) Instead of school administrators arguing with parents, the parents became allies in a common cause. This changed everything. The principal and parents took that school from a chaotic environment to a pearl in the school district, breaking records of academic achievement and with low recidivism rates of kids returning to the school after they went back to a traditional campus.

Of course, it wasn't solely the new school government that effected this change. More importantly, it was the way school faculty interacted with the kids. Similar to the way I had once seen juveniles who wouldn't behave, the teachers and administrators saw the kids as troublemakers. When the teachers asked what they could do to change, I told them.

"I want you to teach these children like they are college students," I said. "In your mind, realize that they are not hooligans but are future doctors and future attorneys."

By changing the paradigm of the adults, we could change the futures of the kids. It's clear to see that if you think a child is a piece of crap, that is all the child will ever be to you. Intentionally or not, you'll treat the child that way verbally and nonverbally, and the message will stay with and damage that child. This concept is often referred to as a self-fulfilling prophecy. But it's more than just a catchphrase. It has deep psychological roots. The Pygmalion concept is a theory that people do better when they are expected to do better. The Golem concept presents the opposite side of that coin: negative expectations lead to negative results. These concepts have been examined and proven in numerous studies, demonstrating that people—adults and children—will live up or down to our expectations.

Charles Cooley was a sociologist who described this same concept as the "looking glass self" back in 1902. He proposed that a child's self-image is established by the age of five, based on how that kid perceives the interactions with the authority figures around him. In other words, the way the world (or parents, teachers, etc.) views a kid determines how that kid sees himself. And that self-image doesn't just last a short period; it lasts for life. That makes it so easy to understand why kids who are treated as if they are unworthy will act like it.

As I considered Cooley's concept, that analogy of the Tree of Love and the Tree of Fear made even more sense. When a kid gets in trouble, parents acting from the Tree of Fear will say things such as, "Why are you always getting in trouble?" or "Why don't you ever listen?" or "What is wrong with you? Are you stupid?" They might demand, "How many times do I have to tell you not to do that?" or "Why can't you be more like your brother?" or "Why are you always causing me headaches?"

Troublemaker. Stubborn. Stupid. Lacking. Is this really the message we want to give to an angry, strapping six-foot-tall man-child who once was that scrunchy-faced infant you cherished in your arms?

Some of us may have come into parenthood unprepared. Perhaps it wasn't planned, or circumstances became much more difficult than anticipated. Some of us may have thought we were prepared but still find the constant demands of parenting draining. There is no real way to sift through to see who is eligible to be a parent and who is not. There is no license required. If there were, my own parents would not have qualified.

But now we're here—responsible for taking care of another person. And whether or not we planned it, or whether or not it's going according to plan, it is still a duty and a privilege to help that person grow up successfully. To do this, we need to understand how we behave as parents. Are we doing what is necessary to help our children grow up mentally, physically, and emotionally healthy, even when times are difficult?

What are our expectations, and are we expecting the best or the worst? What's the message we're sending to the young ones in our lives? Is it the one we mean to send, and if not, how can we change it? Can we learn to listen to the messages others send to our children so we can intercede if they're the wrong ones? Can we figure out how to do better?

We need to remember that our children are not just like us. They form their own ideas and beliefs; they have their own dreams and desires. Getting to know who our own children are is a thing many parents forget to do—but it is one of the most essential steps we can take to create lasting change. And, with a little help from some psychologists, I can show you how.

ARE WE TAKING CARE OF OUR KIDS' NEEDS BEYOND THE BASICS?

MASLOW KNOWS WHAT YOU NEED

CHAPTER 9

HOW DO WE LEARN HOW TO UNDERSTAND ONE ANOTHER? First, we have to understand each other's needs. After all, our actions are guided by our innate desire to fulfill those needs. When our children behave in ways we don't understand, they are most likely seeking something they need. Sometimes this is conscious. Other times, they may not even be aware of the need they are trying to fulfill—but the drive toward it is powerful just the same. That's one of the first things I explain to parents who take part in the VIDA class.

"What are our most basic needs?" I ask, looking around the room to encourage them to yell out answers.

"Food," one parent might call out from the back of the classroom. "Water!"

"Sleep!" Heads around the room nod in agreement.

"Those are all correct. They are some of the most basic needs that humans have. We all need to breathe, eat, drink, and sleep. If these needs aren't met, nothing else matters. But once those are met, we begin to need more. What do you think that might be?"

This time, there's a longer pause.

"Safety," someone might say. That person is right. Once our basic biological needs have been met, being safe—both physically and emotionally—is our top need. As a kid, I knew the cost of not feeling safe. Even though I had a home and didn't worry about where I was going to sleep at night—at least until I was seventeen—I didn't feel emotionally safe, because I never knew whether my mom would be in a rage or not.

"Abraham Maslow was a psychologist who mapped out what humans need." I point to the whiteboard that has a picture of a triangle. "He described it as a pyramid of needs. Maslow's hierarchy starts with the basic physiological needs. Once those have been satisfied, the next step is satisfying the needs for safety, love and belonging, esteem, and finally self-actualization, or living our lives to the fullest. But those top areas of growth cannot occur if the needs at the bottom haven't been met."

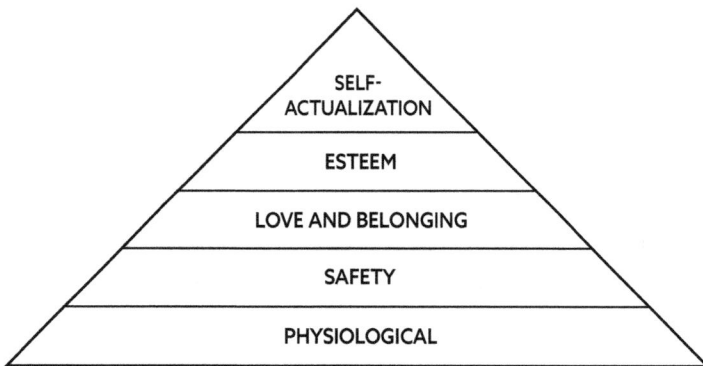

SELF-ACTUALIZATION
ESTEEM
LOVE AND BELONGING
SAFETY
PHYSIOLOGICAL

I check the room to make sure everyone is engaged. It's tricky teaching the psychological concepts when parents so often want to get right to the action steps. But unless they understand and accept the fundamental underpinnings, they will never genuinely embrace a different way of relating with their children.

"It's easy to imagine that people will do whatever they need to do for those bottom level needs. They are essential. If a person stole money to feed his family or crept into a vacant house to stay warm, we'd understand, right?" Various parents in the conference room nod.

"But what about what people will do for needs higher up in the hierarchy? What would people do for friendship or for positive self-esteem? Would it make sense for someone to do almost anything to achieve that?" I ask.

Usually, one parent questions this. "Well, no," that person might say.

But why not? It's the same type of need. Parents often don't understand this—how their children can be driven toward something violent and destructive in search of fulfilling a positive human need such as connection. But the truth is, the human need for connection is so strong, it can override what we consider to be common sense. And in fact, when you think about it, it actually does make sense. Most kids that come through our doors say that they joined a gang for a feeling of belonging, of family. They also wanted to be respected, even if that respect came from intimidating others. When a child's essential needs aren't being met at home, is it any wonder that he is vulnerable to whoever offers to satisfy those needs?

A few years ago, I sat down with a girl named Julia. She was a sixteen-year-old prostitute who had been picked up for solicitation. Slightly heavy, with dark hair, she didn't seem like a typical runaway. She wasn't strung out, and she didn't look desperate.

"We're going to take you back home, Julia," I explained, sitting across from her in my office.

"I'm just going back to Ronnie as soon as I get out of there," she said belligerently, talking about her pimp.

"Why would you go back to Ronnie? Did he threaten you if you left him?" I asked, already planning to have a little talk with Ronnie.

Julia shook her head. "Ronnie takes care of me."

"That's what your parents are for, Julia," I said. "And without you having to prostitute yourself!"

Again, Julia shook her head. "It's just sex, Deputy Cripe. It doesn't mean anything. Besides, Ronnie cares about me. Definitely more than my parents ever did."

"What do you mean?" I asked. "They've been looking for you for months."

"They only care that I'm not there," Julia said. "They don't care about *me*, personally. They always tell me what I've done wrong. They tell me I'm no good or lazy. They don't love me. I don't think they even like me. Nothing I do makes them happy. But Ronnie is happy with me. He says I'm pretty and that I look good. He says I'm one of his favorite girls because I'm willing to do whatever he needs," Julia explained.

Even as bile churned in my stomach at the thought of this pimp taking advantage of Julia's neediness, it made sense. Pimp Ronnie was fulfilling Julia's needs more effectively than her parents. While they may have taken care of her biological needs, they didn't meet the ones higher on the pyramid, like her need to feel loved or to feel good about herself. But Ronnie did. So she was willing to stand on a street corner and have sex with strangers because Ronnie would be happy with her. How messed up is that?

Michael was a fourteen-year-old boy in the VIDA program. He was frequently getting in trouble at school—small things in the big picture but still disruptive, like talking back to teachers and getting into minor scuffles. In his first weeks in the program, Michael's behavior was no different. I asked him to walk away from the group with me into an unoccupied office so I could hear his story. Protecting a child's dignity is extremely important. If I am going to have an open and honest conversation with a child, it's most likely not going to take place where peers can hear. Children must know I care before they care about what I know, so creating spaces that protect dignity is important.

"Michael, it seems like you've had a hard time settling in," I began. I tried to maintain eye contacted with his sad teenaged eyes.

His small shoulders shrugged as he nervously picked at his fingernails.

I let the silence settle around us as I sat down in an office chair, waiting for his response. After a moment, Michael sat down in the chair opposite mine.

He looked up at me almost expressionlessly. "It doesn't matter. I won't be here long." His tone was cold and distant.

"Why do you think that?" I asked. The program is sixteen weeks, and only a few of those had passed since Michael joined us.

"I never get to stay anywhere. You'll get tired of me, say I'm too much trouble, and ship me off somewhere else," he said.

It is important for kids to see our emotional reactions in our expressions. We all look into faces to see if someone really cares or if they are just going through the motions. Adults often forget that children need to see our emotions—not just hear them. It's easy to show emotion when the feeling is anger, but how do we express love or concern? I let my concern and confusion show through furrowed brows, offering a few seconds of silence while I considered Michael's words. Despite this boy's dispassionate tone, he was clearly hurting. What didn't I know about him that I needed to know in order to reach him? I searched my memory for what I had seen weeks ago in his application.

"You're in a foster home, right, son?" I asked a little more gently.

He nodded, looking at me challengingly, already guarded against rejection.

"How are they treating you there?"

"Okay. They're all right."

"Have you been there long?" I asked.

"Three months."

"And where were you before that?"

He snorted. "Which time?"

"How many foster homes have you been in before this?"

"Well, let's see." He drew out the answer. "Before this current placement? Forty-seven."

Holy shit! This fourteen-year-old had been in almost fifty foster homes! That was more than three for every year he'd been alive! How could anyone feel safe, secure, loved, and important with such constant upheaval? It was a miracle that he wasn't taking drugs, stealing, or worse.

I have often heard stories of babies whose mothers don't bond with them when they are born. The moms may have fed them and changed their diapers, but they didn't soothe the infants when they cried, didn't coo over their smiles, didn't talk or sing to them. Those babies don't develop the deep sense of security they need, and it affects them all of their lives. Who had bonded with Michael? Not just when he was a baby, but in any of those forty-seven, now forty-eight, foster homes where he had lived? Who had told him he was clever, funny, or special? Had anyone ever told him they were glad he was living with them? At that moment, I wished I had a gigantic ranch, with room for all of these kids to live, where I could make sure they would be loved and taken care of as long as they needed.

"Well, Michael, sorry to disappoint you, but you're not going anywhere. You're staying in this program," I said sternly.

Michael looked at me, hesitation in his eyes.

"Michael." I met his gaze, willing him to absorb my words. "You matter. You matter to me. I like you, and I want you to stay here so we can work together."

It took some time and repetition, but over the course of the VIDA program, Michael began to understand that he indeed did matter. He began to realize that he was wanted. His grades began to improve, and his teachers and foster parents said his behavior was angelic. All he needed was to feel safe and loved and as though he belonged. Then his self-esteem could grow.

We all crave more than just the fulfillment of basic needs. People will do seemingly dangerous, destructive, or irrational things to get those additional needs met. As parents, teachers, and communities, instead of looking at these kids as troublemakers, can we look at them and understand that their behaviors are actually logical attempts to fill a psychological well? With that insight comes the hard question: are we taking care of our kids' needs, beyond the basics? Are we doing it consistently? How do we make our children feel important, feel loved, and feel that they matter? How can we breathe this belief into them?

Maslow's hierarchy helps explain that some behaviors are inherent, given the environment, which provides the framework for many situations I see. But there are several more frameworks to understand as we work with kids. The more I can understand psychological theories like Maslow's, the better I can get to the kids' underlying motivations and begin to really help. And so can you.

We must

UNDERSTAND THE

BELIEF

BEHIND THE

BEHAVIOR

REALITY CHECK
THROUGH THE
REALITY MODEL

CHAPTER 10

JUST AS WE ALL HAVE NEEDS, WE ALL HAVE BELIEFS, OR OUR OWN REALI-
TIES—ONES THAT GUIDE US THROUGH LIFE AND HELP US MAKE SENSE OF THE
WORLD. According to the Franklin Reality Model, we only hold on
to the beliefs we "know" to be true, and we are in a constant state of
writing and rewriting those "truths." We usually assume that they
are helpful, but sometimes, they're not. Sometimes, our beliefs limit
us from our potential.

I have heard "I can't" countless times from people I work with—
kids *and* adults. That statement even invades my thinking, especially
when I let fear begin to control my thoughts. This was a huge lesson
for me when I started to lead rock climbs. My exposure to risk was
greater, and therefore I had to learn to fight my own fears. For me,
rock climbing became my forge. A place and time for me to either
accept what I thought I could not do or to change my belief in myself and become that which I dreamt of being.

I remember a moment twenty years ago when I was ascending
a perfect granite slab known as the Apron in Yosemite Valley with
some skilled climbers. They had roped up a climb that looked very
challenging because it was steep with only tiny edges to grab onto
and a thin vertical crack. Picture a butter knife laid sideways on your
table, and you have to hold onto the thin blade part—that's what

I mean by thin. I kept asking the others what the climb was rated, and they would not tell me. I told them that I could only climb a certain difficulty rating; in this case, it was 5.10c. The 5 indicates a vertical roped accent, and the .10c declares the size of holds and overall difficulty. Each number has four letter ratings; for example, 10a, 10b, 10c, and 10d, and then it jumps to 5.11a. They smiled, and one of them said, "Well, then, you should do just fine on this." I tied into the rope and started to climb. The route was steep, but I loudly and fearfully proclaimed that I could only climb a 5.10c, and my companions wouldn't let me climb something for which I was not prepared, so I pressed on. Every muscle strained as I pulled myself to the top. After I reached that peak and was lowered back to the ground, I looked at the others climbers and asked breathlessly, "Okay, what is it rated?"

They all laughed. "That thin crack you just did is a 5.11c."

No way! I thought. *I can't climb that hard a route. I never have.* "Show me the climbing book where this is rated," I demanded. I believed more in what I could *not* do than what I *could* do—so much so that I had to make up a reason for this freakish occurrence before I accepted the fact that maybe, just maybe, I was more capable than I thought!

Later, as a rock-climbing instructor, hearing the words "I can't" from climbers told me right where they were mentally. And as I watched them inch their way up the hundred-foot slabs, I knew they were rewriting their beliefs right before my eyes. Lifelong paradigm shifts were occurring, and in support of them, I asked my students to delete "I can't" from their vocabulary. They could say "It's difficult" or "I'm scared" instead. Those statements can be confronted, and in the end, that shift makes a huge difference in how we proceed in life and how we climb a mountain.

What does this mean when we talk about kids? Their beliefs guide their behaviors. Remember Michael, the boy shuffled between forty-eight foster homes? What do you think his beliefs were? I think he believed he was unworthy of acceptance, that he was a bad kid and nobody would want him. His belief was understandable, because his history had proven it "true." He even behaved in ways to make it true. But when offered a different outcome—the idea that he would not be rejected, that we were not going to let him go—he had to rethink his belief.

Same thing with David, the teenager who didn't see the point of going to school because he assumed he would be dead soon anyway. His belief made sense, but it wasn't necessarily true. By challenging him with the concept of a different future, we helped him question that initial belief. Over the years, it amazed me how many kids stated that I was the first adult to tell them, to yell, "You matter, your life matters, and your dreams matter!" I have often wondered why it is that I, a law enforcement officer, am the first person saying this to these kids.

So, what exactly is the Franklin Reality Model? Hyrum Smith, founder of the Franklin Quest Company and creator of the Franklin Planner productivity system, described how our beliefs influence our lives. Smith said that we all filter events through a lens that is actually our belief structure.

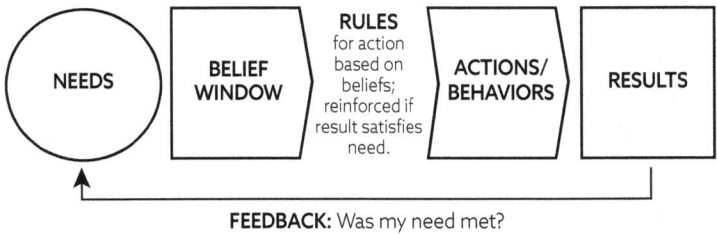

FEEDBACK: Was my need met?

How we interpret events through our belief window provides the rules for behavior. If the results meet our needs, we repeat the process. Let's say we have a need to be safe, which we all do (remember Maslow's hierarchy of needs), and on my belief window, I have a belief that all dogs bite. What behavior might I choose when I see a dog? Whatever behavior I choose, I will measure the result. So let's say I run. If the dog does not bite me because I ran, I met my safety need, right? Now I can write a new belief on my window without challenging my old one: running away from dogs works!

NEEDS	BELIEF WINDOW	RULES for action based on beliefs; reinforced if result satisfies need.	ACTIONS/ BEHAVIORS	RESULTS
I need to be safe.	I believe that all dogs bite.		I choose to run.	I did not get bitten.

FEEDBACK: Yes, my need for safety was met.
The rule to run upon encountering a dog was reinforced and is likely to be repeated, and a new belief is created.

We have so many beliefs that guide us that we rarely examine them to see if they're true. There's an old tale about a young bride who is preparing a roast, and before she puts it in the pan, she cuts off a piece at either end. Her husband asks her why, and she explains that was the way her mother always did it. The bride then asks her mother why she cuts off the meat, and the mother explains that it's the way *her* mother did it. The grandmother finally solves the mystery: at the time when *she* was cooking a roast, the pan was too small, and cutting off the ends was the only way the meat would fit! An amusing example, perhaps, but illustrative of how we can behave certain ways based on beliefs we never question.

When I was a young kid, my mother warned me not to touch drywall because the dust was acidic. Most likely, she didn't want me traipsing drywall dust from nearby construction projects into the house. But even as a young man, I believed her words, warning construction co-workers to use gloves to protect themselves from injury when picking up drywall. They laughed and assured me it was safe. But I didn't believe them. Finally, one of them actually rubbed some of the dust on my arm. I braced myself for the burn, but it didn't come. If it didn't burn, it must not contain acid. If the drywall didn't have acid, the belief I had held for nearly twenty years was wrong! Once I understood that, I no longer avoided drywall or insisted upon wearing gloves when I touched it. My belief had changed, so my behavior changed. Of course, this discovery led to a new, more disturbing belief: my mother lied! That new belief took me on a journey to re-examine everything she ever taught me or told me. I realized that some of the "truths" I had written on my belief window were, in fact, false. Today, I am very careful not to believe something just because someone tells me it is true. I weigh it and measure it. If I am going to add it as one of my beliefs, I need to make sure it's as accurate as possible.

The same concept works when we want to change a kid's behavior. We must first understand the belief behind the behavior before we start messing with it. After all, maybe it is *our* belief that is wrong and not the child's.

This concept of listening to a child's story before we try to redirect a behavior is a completely different approach than assuming we know more than the child and demanding that the child align with *our* truth. The latter is often the go-to method for parents or adults attempting to change a child's behavior. Programs like "Scared Straight" assume that if we can fill a child with fear, it will result in long-term behavioral changes. But it doesn't work. Think about when you're driving down the highway, going ten or fifteen miles above the speed limit. You see a patrol car parked on the side of the road. What do you do? Slow down, of course, with your heart racing as you hope you don't get pulled over. Sure, your behavior changes for the moment. But after you breathe a sigh of relief that you were not noticed, your speed creeps up again within the next five miles. That's what we've found in youth programs that intend to show kids the dark side, hoping the negative picture will make them say, "Oh, no, this is not the life for me." Fear only briefly changes their behavior, and only while the fear-inducing element is present. More importantly, given many of these kids' belief structures, these programs don't work because they affirm that this is exactly where they are headed. Kids who have been told all their lives that they are no good and that they don't matter start to believe the hype. Why *wouldn't* they end up in juvenile detention or prison?

Instead of reinforcing this negative belief, we have to replace it with an alternate belief. We have to introduce an idea that is so contrary to the one they currently possess that the two ideas cannot reside side by side; one has to be dismissed. For me, I knew that acid burned. But the white powder on my arm didn't, so it couldn't be acid. Therefore, I had to reject the belief that drywall contained acid. This idea of pushing out one belief in favor of another is exactly what happens with many of the climbers I guide. They realize that, despite their belief that they can't climb, they are actually up higher than they were in the beginning; therefore, they *can* climb!

What we are after is an approach that communicates that a child's life and dreams matter while redirecting negative behaviors toward the positive. To do that, we must listen. This is where our questions become important.

As we reestablished VIDA and explored the basic psychological principals that helped lay its foundation, I learned that there was a technical term for the mind's inability to house two conflicting beliefs at once: cognitive dissonance. Cognitive dissonance is a theory by psychologist Leon Festinger, who found that when we hold two conflicting cognitions (thoughts, beliefs, values, etc.), it creates discomfort, and we look for a way to manage that discomfort. To do so, we may dismiss one or make it less important, accepting the other one.

For those of us who want to change the behavior of young people, that means we need to introduce new cognitions to kids that lead them to a different belief and, thus, a different behavior. For the child who has formed a belief that he is stupid and lazy, being reminded of his accomplishments and of his enthusiasm and energy for things he cares about causes cognitive dissonance. Over time, he begins to develop a different picture of who he is. For the child who believes she is not important, showing her that she matters by highlighting her contributions to a team, trusting her with responsibilities, or affirming every little success causes cognitive dissonance.

These lessons ring true for me when I look back at my own childhood. Both my brother Jerry and I were told repeatedly that we were stupid and would not amount to anything. Our father constantly berated us. Maybe he thought his criticism would be motivating, but it only made us hate him more. When we felt worthless, we acted worthless. I am thankful for the outside influences that gave me a different picture of myself—a picture that I *did* matter and I *could* achieve. Jerry and I have talked a lot about our youth, and we both realize that we have lived our lives in a way that proved Dad wrong. Dad had told Jerry that he was too stupid to be an electrician, but Jerry became an electrician despite Dad's negativity. Me? Well, I set out to help kids who were mislabeled, misunderstood, and mismanaged. Our statements, verbal and nonverbal, have a huge impact on our children's beliefs and their lives.

Cognitive dissonance is not a one-hit cure. We have to continue introducing positive, affirming views of our children so they form new beliefs to counter the years of alternate negative ones they have maintained. One psychologist says it takes one thousand "Atta boys" to counter just one "You're worthless and no good."

What are our kids' beliefs about the world? What do they believe about themselves? What do we say and do that reinforces or counters those beliefs? If we take the time to understand why our kids think the way they do, we have a much better chance of showing them new ideas that make them want to change. What is it that you want your children to hear? How are you communicating to them that they are valued and that they matter?

ACKNOWLEDGE

your BLIND SPOTS

OPENING THE JOHARI WINDOW

· CHAPTER 11 ·

MANY PARENTS WHO TAKE PART IN THE VIDA PROGRAM ARE FACED WITH CHALLENGES THAT ARE VERY COMMON TODAY. They love their children. They want what's best for them. They are parenting the best they know how. But as children get older and the world becomes more complicated, it becomes trickier to parent effectively. Just as we don't need a license to become a parent, few of us attend parenting classes once our children are born! Sure, we can pick up a parenting book or magazine, but those are mostly dedicated to our children's behavior, not necessarily to our own.

That missing piece doesn't always become evident until something goes wrong in the parent/child relationship. When that happens (or ideally, *before* that happens), we have to step back and look at those basic needs all people have and seek the source of our child's behavior. It doesn't necessarily have to be a big secret why your children are behaving the way they are. In fact, if you ask them, they just might tell you.

"But my son won't talk to me," one dad told me in frustration after a VIDA session ended.

"What do you mean, he won't talk to you?" I asked.

"I mean, he won't speak to me. If I walk into the room, he walks out," he said.

"What does your son say when you talk to him?"

The dad shook his head. "I don't even try anymore. He doesn't talk to me, and I don't talk to him."

"How long has this been going on?" I asked.

The dad looked sheepish. "Two years."

Two years? The boy was in his mid-teens, struggling to define himself as a man, and the person you'd think would be his role model had, in effect, exiled him from the family! Obviously, something had caused the initial rift, and both father and son were undoubtedly hurting and missing having a relationship. Although it might take more intensive counseling to help them completely rebuild their bond, they could still begin to take those steps to become closer, even after two years of estrangement.

After parents begin to understand Maslow's hierarchy of needs and Franklin's Reality Model, it does little good unless they can put those theories into action. But communicating with their kids is often the difficult part for parents whose interactions with them have devolved into nagging, arguing, yelling, and worse. They need a new way to communicate, a way that helps both sides learn to listen, to trust, and to disclose information, knowing that what they say will be accepted and respected.

That's why I tell parents about the third and last psychological concept: the Johari Window. This model helps improve self-awareness, trust, and communication. The simple diagram has four areas.

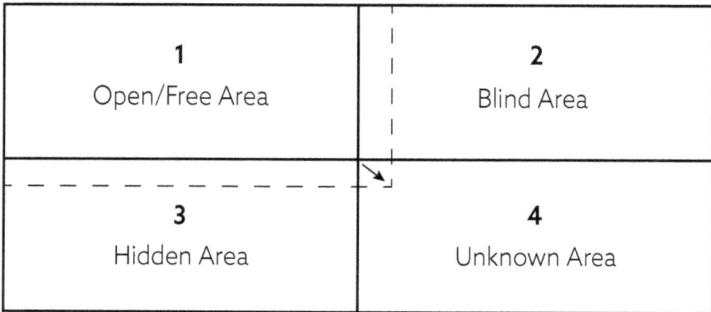

1 Open/Free Area	2 Blind Area
3 Hidden Area	4 Unknown Area

AREA 1, OPEN/FREE AREA: information about a person that is known by others. For example, you may have an outgoing personality. You enjoy entertaining others with stories of your adventures. Others around you know you like to talk and laugh.

AREA 2, BLIND AREA: information that others know about you but of which you're unaware. You may not realize that others have a hard time engaging in a conversation with you because they can't get a word in—you do all the talking.

AREA 3, HIDDEN AREA: information you know about yourself but others do not. Others may not realize that you talk so you're not seen as shy and insecure, which is how you feel about yourself.

AREA 4, UNKNOWN AREA: information that neither you nor others know, such as positive or negative aspects that have not yet come to surface.

When we want to establish a relationship with our children that embodies trust, respect, and open communication, it's obvious that we want Area 1 of the window to be as wide open as possible. There we can have the kind of two-sided conversation that moves past conflict and helps both sides connect and understand each other. The way to get that window open wider is to squeeze into one of the other areas, primarily Areas 2 and 3. To better understand our children, we need to be willing to ask them about our own blind area. What do they know about us that we're not aware of but that is most likely affecting our relationship? We also need to invite our children to share with us more, allowing us to go into the hidden area of the window. What do our children feel or need that they aren't saying?

Imagine the Johari Window of the son who hadn't spoken with his father for two years. How open do you think his window was? What areas of his life—his hopes, his dreams, his fears—were hidden? If we look back at Maslow's hierarchy, we know that the boy, like the rest of us, had essential needs. One of the needs was for family, friends, and a sense of belonging. If he wasn't getting that from his father, who was providing it? How could the father find out if he and the boy never spoke?

I like the Johari Window because it asks parents to think beyond their own beliefs—exploring the blind area. As adults, we have learned hard life lessons and experienced great successes. We have wisdom that comes with age, and if our kids would only do what we tell them to do, we are convinced that everything would turn out right. That thinking, although understandable, often puts us right in the blind area. We neglect to realize that our kids think differently than we do, the world works differently than it did when we were kids, and we may actually not have all the right answers.

My son, Matt, was about seventeen when he declared he wanted to be a video game designer.

"That's ridiculous. You can't make a future in that," I said. Without a word, Matt disappeared into his room, only to emerge soon after with several pieces of paper. He had researched the industry and found that one of the new games out at the time, Halo, had amassed millions of dollars in revenue in its first day of sales. Video game design was a burgeoning area, and although I thought it was a silly career, I was wrong. I was also lucky: my son felt secure enough with me to refute my statement. But what if he hadn't? My initial reaction and my assumption that I was correct in all things could have broken down communication as my son tried to share his excitement and enthusiasm for his career choice. How long before he might feel comfortable sharing anything with me again? What if he had a problem that he was scared of or ashamed of—what were the chances he'd come talk to me?

To increase communication, to open up the Johari Window, we parents need to become more aware of our blind side, which can be done in two simple steps. First, remember that we don't know everything—even when we think we do. That recognition opens the possibility for other ideas, other perspectives. And second, ask questions. Even when a child comes to you with a question of his own, instead of rushing in with an answer, consider asking a question in return. Even if you think you know the answer, you may not. Most parents assume they know their child inside and out. After all, in most cases, the child shares your DNA, and you have been with the child since day one. But children are individuals with their own perceptions and ideas, which may be very different from yours. Unfortunately, parents tend to get offended when their child, their very flesh and blood, thinks or acts differently than what that parent expects. "What do you mean, you don't want to play sports? Of course you do. I played sports. Your brothers played sports. Why don't you?" Or imagine a growing, thinking teenager whose political views differ greatly from her parents. The object of parenting is to help children become thoughtful, kind contributors to the world— not just to create little versions of you. But when they dare to have different views and, worse yet, to express them, we tend to shut them down. Instead, we need to encourage them to be independent, to articulate their reasons, and to consider thoughtfully the details of their ideas. And we do that by suspending our own opinions and beliefs and asking them more about theirs.

Of course, in the process, we may learn something we were happier not knowing. I remember sitting around a campfire one night in the backcountry as an observer while a younger instructor led the nighttime exercise. The group consisted of eighth graders and a teacher from a Christian school. It was a typical evening, and we challenged the kids to share things from their own lives. As time went on, the instructor asked a young girl to share. As the girl started to talk, she began to cry. Through the dim firelight, I could see her face broadcasting a great deal of pain. I listened intently as the questions and answers went back and forth like a ping-pong match.

"I've never told anyone this," the girl said in a voice that barely carried over the flow of the nearby stream.

"Told anyone what?" the instructor asked.

"I shouldn't say," she hesitated.

"You're safe here," the instructor promised. "Whatever you want to say is okay."

The girl glanced around and straightened slightly, becoming visibly bolder. "It's about what my father did to me."

"What do you mean?" the instructor asked gently.

"He raped me," she said, crossing her arms in front of her chest and rocking slightly back and forth.

Silence fell as everyone stared at the ground.

"Well, um, I think we'll stop here for the time being," the instructor said. He and the teacher immediately stepped away and whispered furiously to each other, trying to figure out what to do next. Neither of them was ready for this type of disclosure. As I watched the girl's reaction to how the adults responded, I worried that her fear would consume her once again and that she would crawl back into that dark place she had just worked so hard to come out of, with her open window closing even more tightly than when they started the exercise. I was a guest in that group, not the one in charge, but I couldn't stand by and do nothing. "That was very brave," I told her, asking her if she was okay. She nodded and appeared to be telling the truth. Then I pulled one of the staff members aside to make sure he would talk with the girl and not let her think her heartfelt confession was unimportant. I also reminded the staff member to follow through on the mandated reporting of child abuse.

When we ask children questions, we'd better be ready to accept whatever comes out of their mouths. And we'd better be able to deal with it calmly and compassionately. Imagine a medical doctor asking you what's wrong, but when you describe your symptoms, he freaks out and runs out of the room. How would that make you feel?

To build a better relationship with our children, we have to be willing to admit we don't know everything and that we each have our blind areas that we'd like to reduce. As we do, we build trust with our children because we are willing to be vulnerable first. My kids know I do not have all the answers, but they also know I will help them find those answers. This is how we keep our open sections expanding.

Area 2 is most important when you think about the things you don't know about your kids. These are the things your kids don't tell you—perhaps because of reasons in your own Area 2—but regardless, this quadrant hosts the needs, worries, fears, hopes, and dreams they may have but don't trust you enough to share. Your child knows he's failing biology, but he doesn't tell you. He fears you'll get angry. He doesn't want to disappoint you. He worries he is stupid. He thinks if he tells you, you won't let him go to his friend's house this weekend. In other words, he doesn't trust that you'll understand, support, or help him. So when you ask him how school is going, he says "fine" but feels an ache in his stomach that comes from the lie.

A young girl, not more than thirteen years old, came into our program and disclosed that she was worried she was pregnant. She refused to tell her parents, but she was terrified. We did not become upset but, rather, remained very calm. We asked her if she would be willing to take a test to find out. She said yes. She wasn't pregnant, but she could have been, and we knew that this was simply step one of what would be a long process of working with her. She was obviously sexually active (and to be active at such a young age screams that some basic need is not being met). For that reason alone, wouldn't parents want to know what is going on so they can help their child navigate this emotional turmoil today and avoid it in the future? What about the teen who is being bullied, receiving hateful messages on his or her cell phone or on social media, but who doesn't trust that Mom or Dad would understand? Or the child who is gay but believes his parents won't be accepting?

When a child has so much stored in the hidden side, how can a parent even begin to crack that barrier? Just as questions help unveil the blind area, questions help start communication in the hidden area.

I suggest to parents that they start with low-risk questions. These are questions that don't have a wrong answer—or at least shouldn't. *Who do you think will win the football game today? Do you like this shirt? What's your favorite color?* Then, after the child answers, follow up with, *That's interesting. Why is that?* Eventually, you can move up to questions that are riskier. *What are you working on in biology? What did you do for lunch today?* Eventually, parents can move to high-risk questions, such as *How are you doing in biology? What do you think you'd like to do after high school? You seem kind of down. How can I help?*

It may take minutes to move from low-risk to high-risk questions, or it may take months, but your questions, even the innocuous ones, invite your child to open up. And each response you give reinforces whether opening up to you was a good idea.

One more thing to consider when looking at the hidden area is that parents have hidden areas, too. When we talked about the Tree of Fear, we saw how our fears and other emotions could create negative behavior that belies our intentions. Some of the greatest conflicts between children and parents originate in areas that are hidden from each other. What may look like a battle of wills, for example, may be something else entirely.

"I'm not going to let her win," a mother will declare vehemently. Win what? What battle is the mother fighting? It may appear to be a battle over how the teen dresses, but the daughter may have a hidden belief that the mother doesn't trust her and treats her like a baby. Contrast that to the mother who is afraid that men will look at the daughter's attire and presume the daughter is older and more sexually experienced. The mom may want to protect the daughter, keep her from getting hurt, but the daughter doesn't want to be controlled. That's a bigger issue than how short a skirt is. Once the mom is willing to share her hidden concerns, she can turn the daughter into an advocate in solving the bigger question. How can the daughter be more independent in how she dresses but still be safe? That's a very different approach than being concerned with winning a round in an argument.

The tools from Maslow's hierarchy of needs, Franklin's Reality Model and the Johari Window form a strong foundation for building and rebuilding relationships with our children. First, we must understand that our children behave the way they do for a reason. Second, we must recognize that our children's perceptions, and therefore their behaviors, are colored by their own beliefs, which may be very different from ours. We cannot measure them on our scale. And third, we need to use the lessons we have learned to communicate with our children, inviting them to help us understand them—and when they do communicate with us, we must give them safety and support in return.

Only then can we make positive changes in our relationships and lives.

Change must start WITH US, the PARENTS.

LESSONS LEARNED

I'M NOT A PERFECT PARENT. NO ONE IS. But I have used my own childhood experiences (more what *not* to do than what *to* do), as well as what I have learned as a wilderness guide and as a deputy sheriff involved in juvenile intervention, to develop some essential steps that all parents can take to improve their relationships with their children, wherever those relationships fall on the spectrum.

In this section, we'll explore seven lessons that establish the foundation for change. Remember, as much as we may want to change the behavior of our children, the initial change must actually start with us, the parents. We can use our understanding of our children's needs, beliefs, and behaviors to create a new dynamic in how we interact with them. As we change our perspective and our behavior, their reactions change, too.

Whether they show it or not, our kids want us to love them unconditionally, to guide them, and to understand them. We must meet those needs before our kids can take another step toward us. Let's figure out how to do that.

LESSON # 1:
DEFINE WHAT REALLY MATTERS AND WHAT SUCCESS LOOKS LIKE

What do you want for your child? What do you want in your relationship with your child? If you're like many parents, you may have been so caught up in the stress and negativity of a bad relationship with your child that you can't easily answer these questions.

Sometimes it's easier to use what I call the Kodak process. Just like with photographs, the negative can help identify the positive. So think about what you *don't* want for your child.

Parents may say they don't want their child to drop out of school, do drugs, join a gang, or get pregnant. Once we identify what we are fighting against, it becomes much clearer to see what we're fighting for. A parent who doesn't want his child to drop out of school *wants* the child to become educated and get a high school degree, which will lead to more opportunities. A parent who doesn't want her child to do drugs or join a gang *wants* the child to be healthy, focused, and free of behaviors that will hold him back. A parent who doesn't want his child to become pregnant *wants* the child to have the chance to explore educational and career opportunities without the tremendous responsibility of teen parenthood.

When parents think about what they don't want, the focus is usually on a behavior, but when the conversation turns to what they *do* want, the issues become much broader. When we look at the positives, we begin describing goals, vision, and character traits. This change from reactive parenting to proactive parenting helps us become clearer on our goal.

Don't just do this in your head: write it out. On a piece of paper, list ten things you don't want for your child. Then, write out ten things that are the direct opposite of the negatives you wrote down. Next, of those positive outcomes that you want for your child, which ones are the most important, at least right now? If you had to pick two or three, which ones would they be? Put an asterisk next to those. They are the ones to focus on, because once you know the most essential changes that need to be made, you can change or create your family's ethos or culture to reflect those changes. What does it mean to be a (insert your last name)? As a parent, you must model your family's beliefs. If it is not important to you, it will never be important to your child.

So, what is important in your family? What's your family's story? What was essential to your ancestors that comes into effect now? Maybe, for example, your ancestors were farmers, where hard work and planning were key. Or, maybe it's not even based on who your family was or even who you are yet, but on who you want to be. "We Johnsons believe in integrity. Johnsons don't steal." Can you imagine how this creates cognitive dissonance in a kid who has just shoplifted from a store? Or "You studied hard for that test. We Petersons take time to prepare so we can do our best." By creating and describing values you want your child and your family to have, you are giving them direction, but more importantly, you're providing a sense of identity, belonging, and pride. I grew up with the standard that Cripes are honest and hardworking. I expanded that ethic with my kids, teaching them that honesty means being full of integrity. As my son grew older, he wanted to know more about who we are as a family, so I took him on a trip back east to Ohio, where many members of my father's family still lived, and he got to see and hear how this ethos has existed for generations in our line of Cripes.

As you do this exercise, try to focus on the positive. For example, "Cripes are honest," as opposed to "Cripes do not lie." The focus should be on the behavior you want, not the one you do not want. *This is who we are.*

Here's the tough part. It's not enough to say it. You *have* to model it *all the time.* If your kids see you using your neighbor's wireless Internet on the sly, or lying, or doing anything, big or small, that goes against your stated belief, you lose credibility. (An aside: if you behave in a way that conflicts with your ethos, handle it the way you would want your children to: own up to it, figure out why it happened, correct it, apologize, and start again.) Put that list, the one that creates your principles, on the door of your refrigerator or tape it on the bathroom mirror—somewhere you and everyone in the family can be reminded of it and encouraged by it each day.

Defining what matters, reinforcing it through your family's ethos or culture, and modeling it creates that first important step of change. When I sat down with my kids to create our family rules, I had only two for the list: I don't want anyone getting hurt, and I don't want things broken. That covered most everything that mattered to me.

LESSON # 2:
LEARN TO COMMUNICATE OPENLY WITH YOUR CHILDREN

Many of us talk *to* our children, and some talk *at* their children. We often don't talk *with* them. Even with the best intentions, conversations turn into lectures and "teachable moments." And in the less positive moments, we talk—or yell—at our kids in frustration and anger. When those things happen, kids have two typical responses: 1) shutting down or 2) yelling back. Even when a child may appear to be listening, if we continue to drone on, self-preservation (and boredom) will cause them to tune out. They simply don't hear what we're saying. And that can make us even angrier. Here comes the shouting!

Let's think about what we're trying to do when we talk to our kids. Do we want to talk, or do we want to hear what they have to say? Remember the dad who said his son hadn't talked to him in two years? Did the dad's sense of loss come because he had so much to say, or was it more that he wanted to understand what was going on in his son's world? Imagine a conversation where a parent and child want desperately to be *understood,* but no one is taking time to *understand*!

Unfortunately, when most of us communicate with our kids, even in good relationships, we tend to go into teaching mode when we could benefit more by going into learning mode. The ultimate goal is to build trust so your child is willing to open the Johari Window to let you know what he's thinking. You don't accomplish that by lecturing.

If we remember that we're seeking understanding, it becomes easier to remember to ask questions. In addition to acquiring insight into our child's mind, asking questions helps the child develop his thought process, stimulating the frontal lobe of the brain. Many of us have asked our kids questions that originate in the Tree of Fear. *What were you thinking? Have you lost your mind? How many times have I told you not to do that?* While these may appear to be questions, they're not legitimate. We ask these things when we're frustrated and angry and when we know, deep down, that no answer is the right one. Our kids know it, too, and understandably respond by shutting down or by shouting back.

When we want to understand, our questions should be phrased and voiced differently. *Can you tell me why you decided to make that choice? How did that work out for you? What were some of your other options when you did that? That decision confuses me—can you tell me what you were thinking about when you made it?*

These questions are not loaded. There are no wrong answers, and they invite the child to evaluate his own behavior. Sometimes, that's enough to get him talking. Sometimes, however, the child will simply shrug his shoulders and say, "I don't know." Our knee-jerk response to this is, "What do you mean, 'You don't know'? Of course you know why you skipped school/got into a fight/failed your class!" What we often overlook, in the middle of our outrage, is that while that child knows the answer, he doesn't trust us with his knowledge. And we're seeking understanding, right? If we're asking questions and getting stonewalled, we need to ask different questions.

Consider this question as an alternative: "When you say you don't know why you skipped school, do you mean you never thought about it or you don't feel safe sharing your answer?" This question opens up the possibility of more conversation. From here, you can ask your child to reflect on his actions now, with hindsight. You can ask what might help make him feel safer answering your question. You're exploring the real issue, rather than getting blocked with the "I don't know." And yet, you're doing it in an encouraging, supportive way that helps build trust so your child can open up a little more.

Take care not to get caught in the power struggle of demanding that your child share something. Instead, provide some time for the child to consider things, and at the same time, reinforce that this is an important topic and that you care. Even more frustrating than the child who insists that he "doesn't know" is the one who won't talk at all. As you sit there in silence, the temptation is to fill that quiet with lecture. Don't do it! Although dead air can be uncomfortable, be patient enough so that the child fills that silence. Try saying something along the lines of, "This really matters to me, so I'm going to take time to sit here so we can discuss it."

It's much easier to communicate with your child when you understand his world. The issues he is exposed to and dealing with are significantly different from the ones when you grew up. From cyber bullying to rainbow parties, kids are exposed to more temptation, more advantages, and more challenges than ever before. How do you educate yourself about your child's world? Who are their friends? Who are their teachers? What do the kids at school dress like and behave like? What is the norm for dating and parties? Kids may not initially be forthcoming with this, thinking they'll get in trouble if they tell too much. But if you're seeking information and understanding, your questions should reflect an explorative, non-judgmental tone. For example, you might say, "It may be I'm old, but I just don't get it. Why do the guys wear their pants so low? What do other kids in your generation think of the style?" Remember, if you're doing most of the talking, you are probably lecturing. Your goal is to get your child to do most of the talking!

While you may not be a gamer or technology junkie, playing video games with your children, watching their favorite television show with them, or asking them to share YouTube videos they like is a non-threatening way to learn about and show interest in what is happening in their world.

Once you've built enough trust that your child is ready to talk, be ready to listen—even if he is sharing things you'd rather not know about. If your teenage daughter wants to talk to you about having sex, please listen. Resist the urge to lecture. Naturally, you're concerned. But what concerns you most? Is it an unplanned pregnancy? I've seen parents in this situation call their daughters sluts and whores and make them feel ashamed and alone. Ultimately, that response often convinces the daughter that she is acting promiscuously, which begins a self-fulfilling prophecy. What if, instead, the parent focused on emphasizing responsibility and helping the daughter figure out her options, how to protect herself, and how to stay safe? What if the questions were, *What do think would happen if you were to get pregnant? What do you think it takes to be able to raise a child? Can you envision your life if that were to happen?* The purpose is to help her think through her decisions and the possible consequences without causing automatic resistance.

Obviously, this is a loaded issue, and it's perfectly fine to tell your child that you believe sex should be reserved for two married people or that you are concerned that she is too young to be in such an intense relationship or whatever your concerns are. Remember that when your child is willing to share information with you, your reaction is key to reinforcing that behavior. You may not like what you hear, and you don't have to agree with it. But responding out of care, concern, experience, and the quest for understanding will make it more likely that your child will keep sharing with you . . . and also listen to what you have to say.

When my son was eighteen, he asked me what I thought about premarital sex. We had a very open and candid conversation. I shared my point of view and explained why I had come to it. He asked several questions, and then the conversation ended. He came back to me after several hours and said, "You know what? I agree with you, and I think I am going to wait like you did." Mind you, I disclosed exactly what I did and did not do. These conversations did not just happen overnight. It took years of modeling behavior, asking questions, and letting my kids just educate me about their life to reach this point of openness.

LESSON # 3:
TEACH THROUGH DISCIPLINE—NEVER PARENT OUT OF ANGER

When are we most likely to dole out *punishment?* When we're still angry with the child for the transgression. And punishment it is. We want to teach that kid a lesson—mostly for the pain, expense, or inconvenience he's caused us. Take away the Xbox. No sleepovers for six months. "You're grounded for a month!" Boy. That kid is really going to be sorry. But when do we take time to teach what a better choice or behavior might have been?

When I was little and my mother beat me breathless, I had no doubt that I was being punished, but many times, I didn't know why. Parents may say that they punish to teach their children to behave, but true punishment doesn't teach. Punishment is an indulgence on the part of parents to vent their frustration in a culturally acceptable way.

Discipline, however, is different. Discipline seeks to both teach a child the error of what happened and provide consequences for the action. It is measured. It is thought out. It is appropriately relative to the transgression, and it is sustainable.

Parents sometimes ask me how they can discipline their child when they are supposed to be asking questions, seeking understanding, and communicating using all of the elements we've been discussing. Discipline is guiding and teaching as well. Kids want to know their parameters, and our job is to show them as we guide them to adulthood. But discipline is separate from the anger or frustration we feel when our child misbehaves.

I advise the parents in VIDA not to discipline a child when they are caught up in emotion. It will surely turn into punishment. Parents sometimes send their kids to their rooms while the consequence is being planned, but the lesson the parent is teaching the child is one of rejection. *You did something wrong, and I can't stand to look at you.* Instead, I suggest that when parents are so angry that they fear saying or doing something hurtful, they give themselves a timeout. Take twenty minutes away from the fray to calm down and think through the real issue or concern. Is it one that goes against your family ethos? Did someone get hurt? Was property damaged? Is this a repeating negative behavior? Were there extenuating circumstances? Do you feel you have listened to the child's perspective and know the whole story? Then, seeing the big picture, you can better assess what may have led your child to behave this way.

Sometimes parents get frustrated with this approach. Why do they have to search for the underlying reason for the misbehavior? Why do *they* have to be the ones who are always reasonable and thoughtful, especially when the kid intentionally does something stupid, selfish, or mean, perhaps repeatedly? I tell parents that somebody has to have the emotional fortitude that a child can anchor to in a storm. That's the role of the parent. Trying to understand your child's perspective, empathizing with him, and communicating with him does not mean you don't provide consequences for negative behavior. But you need to consider those consequences carefully so that they help the child learn.

One boy in VIDA, after several incidents, was warned that if he got into trouble with the law, he would have to leave our program and go to probation camp. Unfortunately, he did get in trouble again, and he was taken into custody. For us, it was a failure because we were not able to help him turn around. Amazingly, however, once he got out of camp and back into school, his behavior was exemplary. We caught up with him months later and asked what changed his perspective and behavior. He said that although he didn't finish the VIDA program, we were the first people to provide consequences and then follow up on them. For the first time, he had a boundary—a reasonable one, and one that was reinforced when he crossed it. That helped establish structure and order for him, and he began to thrive.

A VIDA parent came to me complaining that her son would not do his chores. "Okay," I said, "tell me what happened."

"He won't unload the dishwasher," the mom complained. "I ask him to unload it, but he won't do it."

I knew unloading the dishwasher was a small complaint in the grand scheme of things, but the boy's refusal to help out in this small way could certainly be frustrating to the mom. I told her that I would talk with the boy.

"Your mom says you're not unloading the dishwasher," I said, after pulling him aside.

He shook his head, irritated. "No, I unload it," he explained. "She got mad because I didn't unload it from left to right."

Now, that didn't make sense. This mom's rule was based on her desire for control, not on the concept of maintaining a well-organized home or responsibility or teamwork. Just as we want our children to pay attention to our rules, we parents need to ensure that our rules make sense.

When my own children were young, the family government they established help determine consequences for misbehavior. Start by establishing the purpose of the rule, such as why your child should come home before curfew (i.e., safety issues, getting enough sleep to stay healthy, having time to complete homework, trustworthiness). Follow by asking suggestions for consequences if the rule is broken. "What do you think is a fair consequence if you miss curfew?" "Why do you think that is fair?" Instead of making it a one-way conversation laying down the law, you are opening the door to communicate what you're really concerned about—the safety of your child. Open your own Johari Window and explain why this issue is important to you. You may still make the final decision on the rule and its consequence, but by having this discussion, your child is more likely to understand the purpose of the rule and respect it, and you're more inclined to establish appropriate consequences that address the reason for the rule instead of ones that help you vent frustration in the moment. This also creates an opportunity for your children to take ownership of the rules and consequences they help create and define.

If you're a parent who has decided to create change after years of struggling with your kids, you should most likely start slowly, taking small steps. Start by changing yourself! You need to honestly and openly talk to your kids about the changes you want to see and the why. You need to model them consistently as you move forward.

LESSON # 4:
FOCUS ON WHAT YOU WANT, NOT ON WHAT YOU DON'T WANT

In Lesson # 1, I talked about using the Kodak process to define what you want for your children and for your family. In looking at the negative, it was easier to define the positive. When it comes to behaviors, it is important to do the exact opposite. Focus on the behavior you want to see from your child, not the one you don't want. Often, parents will ignore, or at least not actively pay attention to, their child unless there is a problem. So what is the logical response of a child who needs parental attention? There's an old adage that bad press is better than no press at all. Children feel the same way. They crave attention even more than they crave approval, so they will do whatever it takes to get you to see them. Instead of spending all of your interactions outlining your child's faults, look for and affirm his positive qualities. As parents, you may be in the habit of expecting and only seeing the negative. Changing that expectation can often change the behavior. Give your children the opportunity to live up, not down, to your expectations. It may need to start as a small affirmation. *I love the way you answered that question so honestly. Great job putting your dishes in the sink. Good for you for getting your homework done.*

Every message can't be solely positive. There will be times when you have to talk about a negative behavior, but even then, you can finish with a positive. *This was probably not your finest hour, and we can work through this. However, I really respect and like the fact that you were honest about what happened.* Or *I love you to death and think you're a great kid. I think you could have made a better choice, and I'd like to talk with you about what you were thinking at the time so I can understand where you were coming from.*

Practice ways to see the best in your child so that you are ultimately sending the message to them that they are *good.* There is a significant difference between a child thinking she's a good kid who made a bad choice and a child thinking she is simply a bad kid.

LESSON # 5:
SHOW YOUR CHILD AFFECTION

It is important to show your child that he or she matters. We do that through our actions, our words, and our tone, but one of the best ways is through physical affection. Let me emphasize: this means appropriate, non-sexual contact. This action needs to be one your child is comfortable with; whether it's a hug or a kiss, a fist bump or a high five, this physical contact emphasizes that you're on the same team. Watch any sporting event and you'll see fist bumps, butt smacks, chest bumps, shoulder knocks, and all sorts of positive physical contact between team members. This doesn't only happen when a player makes a good move. In a tennis match, doubles teammates will give each other a low five even if one of them nets the ball, signifying, "Okay, let's reset and start again."

This affection shouldn't be weird, and what your child was comfortable with at a younger age may not fit now. Sitting in Mom's lap for a snuggle may have been fine at age four, but your eleven-year-old is less likely to want that, or at least is less likely to admit to it. Lots of parents kiss babies on the lips, but as the kids get older, one or both of the parents may become less comfortable with that form of affection, particularly when the parent and child are of the opposite gender.

One parent in VIDA told me that she didn't know how to be affectionate with her son, who was a young teen. She was a single mom with several daughters, and she didn't know how to be physically comfortable with her only boy, so she did not touch him. Ever. Can you imagine how it felt not to ever get a pat on the back or head, or an arm around the shoulder, or a kiss on the forehead?

On the other hand, just because a child doesn't seek physical contact doesn't mean he or she doesn't crave it. Desire for human connection is wired into all of us, and children will seek it from some source if they don't get it from you.

If you're not used to having physical contact with your child, start with small gestures. Give your child a brief pat on the arm or knee. Rub her back. Give him a quick squeeze. Kiss her goodnight, even if she's asleep. If your child asks what you're doing, tell him you love him and just wanted to show it.

LESSON # 6:
TURN CONFLICTS INTO OPPORTUNITIES TO LEARN

Conflict is natural, but we tend to shy away from it because it makes us uncomfortable. As parents, we think that when our kids question our decisions, they are being disrespectful. Kids think that when we won't let them do what they ask, we're being too restrictive. Parents worry about losing control, and kids worry about never getting it. Many parents try to protect their children from the world when we should be equipping our children to safely navigate it instead.

A thirteen-year-old yells at her parents that they treat her like a baby because they want her to go to bed at nine thirty. The parents yell back that the girl argues with everything they say and that she *is* acting like a baby. Stalemate. It's natural for our kids to push the parameters, so parents should try not to take it personally when kids question their decisions. It means they are developing into critical thinkers. What if instead of insisting on staying in control, the parents acknowledge that their daughter is right; at the age of thirteen, she should have some input about her bedtime. What if the parents explain that they're concerned she gets enough rest to be alert at school and that she not crash as soon as she comes home? What if the parents ask for the daughter's ideas on how that could happen? Suddenly, instead of not listening (and, in the daughter's eyes, not caring), the parents work with the girl to become problem solvers.

Instead of going into full-scale defensive mode, it's often more effective to go into a questioning mode. Encouraging your child to think through the issue helps her gain the skills needed to find a solution instead of just being defensive. Too often, we want to give the child the answer, and when we do that, she has a tendency to rebel, but when she discovers her own answer, she's more likely to accept it.

We have kids in our program who think they don't need to finish high school to live in a nice middle-class neighborhood and drive a nice car; they think working at a fast food restaurant as a fry cook is all it will take. Nothing we can say will change their minds, so we have them do an exercise instead. They make a grocery list, based on what they'd like to buy, and look up those prices. Then we look at rent and housing prices to see what they could afford on their fast food salary. Without being *told* that these choices will not produce the lifestyle they desire, the kids begin to realize (through cognitive dissonance) that without a basic education, their options are limited.

Once, several boys in the program told me they aspired to be drug dealers. (It was an indication of the trust between us that they would even start this conversation with me.) Drug dealers made money, they explained. True, I agreed. But what about rival drug dealers? How would the boys handle them as a threat? Obviously, I wasn't going to help them problem-solve this issue, but instead of telling them that the idea was ridiculous or dangerous, I used the conversation as a chance to help them come to that conclusion on their own.

Sometimes the conflict is created on purpose. Remember the woman who called the police because her daughter had taken twenty dollars out of the mom's purse? Why did the daughter do it? According to the mom, the daughter wasn't even trying to sneak it out. She walked over to her mother's purse, took it out, and wouldn't give it back until the police arrived. So, what is this really all about? Why did the girl so flagrantly take the money if she were going to refuse to give it back? Could it be that she wanted her mother's attention and was willing to do anything possible to get it? Instead of focusing on the twenty dollars, look further and find out the reason for the action.

At times, parents and children will simply disagree. A teen wants to go to a party, and the parent is not comfortable with it. Maybe it will be unsupervised or at a house where underage drinking is likely. The teen promises that he won't be drinking and that of course he'll behave, but the parent, after evaluating underlying concerns about the boy being in a possibly unsafe scenario, still says no. That's fair. There's a difference between a knee-jerk negative reaction and a thoughtful, considered response that perhaps even ties back to the family ethos. Parents don't have to cave when they disagree with their child, and they can use the opportunity to help the teen think about consequences he may not have considered. *What do you think might happen if underage kids are drinking and the police show up? If the party isn't supervised, what do you think will happen if people who weren't invited show up? Or if a fight breaks out? What if someone gets hurt?*

Parents can also offer options. "I know you wanted to go to this party, but you know my concerns. Is there anything we can do to help alleviate them?" Perhaps someone can supervise the party after all, or the son can do something different. It may not be the solution your son was hoping for, but it offers a compromise that recognizes your valid concerns and is respectful to the son's wishes.

LESSON # 7:
HANDLE A CRISIS WITH LOVE

It's easier to envision being understanding, asking good questions, listening thoughtfully, and being a better parent when life is going smoothly. But when a crisis arises, it is challenging to recall all of the positive behaviors and put them to work. Your child was just arrested for shoplifting, and you're supposed to stop and figure out which of her basic needs weren't being met? Your son was expelled for fighting, and you're supposed to come to him from the Tree of Love? Your daughter snuck out of the house to be with her boyfriend, and you're supposed to ask her non-judgmental questions?

It's much more familiar to fall back into those previous parenting behaviors and beliefs. *Why didn't he listen to me? Why does she always do this? That kid is nothing but trouble!*

As nice as it would be to assume that once you've begun using the parenting techniques we've talked about, everything will go smoothly, that's not reality. You may have many bumps in the road. But how you address them, how *you* navigate a crisis, will go far in solidifying or straining the relationship you have with your child.

If you get a call telling you your child is in trouble, the first thing to do is assess the crisis. Is your child safe and uninjured? If that is the case, you have more opportunities to help your child recover. Are others involved, and are they safe? If everyone is okay, the immediate threat is lowered and you can take a moment to find out what the situation is.

Even knowing the situation, though, does not always tell you the whole story. Your child got into a fight. Why? What caused it? Was your child being picked on? Was your child defending someone? Was your child picking on someone else? Your child may be at fault, but even so, it is important to think about what precipitated that behavior. Kids may act out at school when there is dysfunction at home. A child who is bullied can also become a bully. Your child was drinking and driving. What led him to drink alcohol? Did he succumb to peer pressure or drink to cover an emotional pain? What is the frequency of the act? Is this a new behavior or a repeated one? If this happens often, it may indicate a more severe issue than if it is a one-off. If it is frequent, when does it occur and around whom? Is there anything that precipitates the behavior, such as an argument with family or friends? There are many questions to be asked before you can truly understand the *what* and *why* behind the action.

Determine the severity of the act. One mom called us and said that her young daughter was becoming a delinquent. We asked what was going on, and the mom said the girl was stealing cookies out of the cookie jar. Some behaviors are just normal kid behaviors. Sneaking cookies, being slow to do chores, and having untidy rooms are to be expected. Thinking this is the end of the world creates much more stress on both you and your child than it should. No parent wants his child to be arrested, but even if that happens, it doesn't sentence your child to a life of crime. Remember that a child will live up or down to your expectations. If you assume that your child is a good kid who made a mistake, your child will hear a very different message than if you believe your child is simply *bad*.

Understand the consequences and start to problem-solve. If your child was arrested, was it for an infraction (i.e., truancy, curfew, etc.), which would allow you to pick him up from the station? Or was it for a misdemeanor (i.e., vandalism, petty theft, etc.), which may require setting a court date, or a felony, which would require hiring a lawyer? If your child was expelled from school, what needs to be done so he or she can return?

The first time you see your child after he or she has gotten into trouble is a deeply emotional moment because so many of your fears and frustrations can bubble to the surface. I caution parents to take a moment in this situation and ask themselves, *How can I navigate this crisis? How can I ensure that whatever I say, love is the loudest thing my child hears?* You may certainly be disappointed, sad, and scared. Your child, despite exhibiting a brave or rebellious face, is probably feeling those emotions, too. Ask yourself if this crisis is worth emotionally damaging your child with your reaction. When would be a better time for you to model to your child how to work through a crisis thoughtfully and lovingly?

While these suggested steps may help you get through a crisis, there isn't one perfect answer to navigating an unexpected predicament. But by keeping your child's emotional well-being at the forefront and reminding yourself to let love speak the loudest, the direction to take will be clearer.

AFTERWORD
LOVE LOUDLY

"I did my best," my father said five years ago as I sat next to his hospital bed. He had been diagnosed with cancer and grudgingly acknowledged that he could use help, even from the son whom he'd declared would never amount to anything. For all of the verbal abuse my father had spewed, for all the times that he'd stood by while my mother physically abused me, and for all of the times that even now, after he's gone, I still feel like a defenseless child, I have compassion for him. He did do his best.

As an adult, I understand that my parents didn't know any better. Coupled with their own history and dynamics and the limited amount of parenting knowledge available, I find forgiveness for their failings. After all, my experiences, good and bad, created the person I am today, the person with a wonderful wife, three terrific children, and a mission to give other parents the education and tools to do better. But even though times have changed, we haven't made enough progress with our kids.

As parents, we are our children's first leaders. We are supposed to guide them in the right direction, teach them and support them so they can have fulfilling, useful lives that contribute to our world. But there's a generation that's getting lost in the shuffle. It's not just kids from certain socioeconomic or ethnic backgrounds. It's not just kids from single-parent homes or kids who live in urban areas. It's not just pre-teens and teenagers. All of our kids are at risk.

When I look around at an incoming class in the VIDA program, when I read a news story about a kid who made a horrible, life-altering mistake or one who was a tragic victim, I know that we're not in the clear. When we have kids who come into the program unprepared to succeed in life because they can't read or have a learning disability that no one has noticed, I see that we're still failing our kids. When parents, who should be their kids' frontline of defense against the world, don't notice their kids' needs, and neither do the teachers, the kids eventually get in trouble. But when they do, our common response is to punish them, not to find out why and how this happened. Not to reach out with understanding and support, but with anger and judgment.

Remember: children do not dream of failing, so rather than judge and condemn, we need to explore those hurts that are causing the behavior and then address what is holding them back in their academic achievement. Then, you've just opened the pathway for them to excel. If a child is failing, it's not just a responsibility but also a moral obligation for the adults around to investigate why.

That is what we try to do at VIDA, but your child doesn't have to be in the VIDA program in order to get that loud love. Your child should get it from you. Now that you have read this book, now that you understand the needs and motivations that are wired into your child, now that you have gained insight into talking, listening, and understanding, you are charged to love your child and those you interact with, loudly.

It's my hope that this book doesn't just change one family. My hope is that it changes millions. That everyone who reads this book looks at the youth around him or her with compassion and a desire to understand more deeply. That everyone pauses before drawing a conclusion or labeling a child as a hooligan and approaches that child from the Tree of Love, not the one grounded in fear. I hope this book starts a movement. A new way of parenting, not just for kids who are in trouble, but for all kids—because each and every one of them can benefit from a loving, understanding relationship with the adults in their lives.

As you've gone through this book, I hope you've seen places where you can make different, better choices as you parent, teach, coach, or work with kids. And I pray that you'll commit to making those choices, ones that will undoubtedly affect those kids throughout their lives.

For more inspiration and ideas, I invite you to join the Love Loudly movement, where we are building a message of a revolutionary way of interacting with others. Child by child, we can make a difference, making sure every one of them knows that he or she matters.

www.loveloudly.org

ABOUT THE AUTHOR

Mark first escaped his dysfunctional and abusive home through backpacking with the local scouting troop, and he left home for good as a seventeen-year-old, enlisting in the U.S. Marine Corp.

After serving in the Marines, Mark went to college to be a marriage counselor but soon developed a desire to work with youth within the faith-based community. This evolved into a focus in education with an emphasis on wilderness experiential education. Mark was a wilderness backcountry guide for several California-based companies working with "at-risk" youth, CEOs, and families. Mark also did a stint as a professional rock climber for Disneyland. Together with his wife (his best friend), Mark backpacked across thirteen countries and was homeless for eight months upon return to the States.

Eventually, Mark found employment with the largest sheriff's department in the world, in Los Angeles County. It did not take long before his assignments steered him toward delinquency intervention. Mark received the prestigious "Leadership and Communication" award from Toastmaster International, and he has been recognized by the California State Senate, the Governor of California, and the United States Congress for his work in juvenile intervention. His focus has gone from street gangs to child abuse to delinquency intervention. Now in his 24th year as a deputy sheriff, Mark has worked the last fourteen years in juvenile delinquency intervention, where he developed a state-certified Juvenile Intervention Instructors Course that has trained numerous community-based leaders and other law enforcement agencies.

Mark continues to work with families in crisis, focusing on the challenges of parenting and spreading the belief that if we can change the way adults communicate, we will change the way kids behave!

www.ingramcontent.com/pod-product-compliance
Lightning Source LLC
Chambersburg PA
CBHW072013090426
42740CB00011B/2171